DSA®
DRIVING STANDARDS AGENCY
SAFE DRIVING FOR LIFE ™

The **OFFICIAL DSA GUIDE** to
LEARNING
TO DRIVE

London: TSO

Written and compiled by the Learning Materials section of the Driving Standards Agency.

© Crown Copyright 2010

Originally known as *Your Driving Test*
First edition 1990
Second edition 1993

Previously known as *The Official Driving Test*
Third edition 1996
Fourth edition 1999
Fifth edition 2001
Sixth edition 2003

New title - *The Official DSA Guide to Learning to Drive*
Seventh edition 2004
Eighth edition 2007
Ninth edition 2009 incorporating 'The Official DSA Guide to Helping Learners to Practise'
Third impression 2010

ISBN 978 0 11 5530913
A CIP catalogue record for this book is available from the British Library.

Other titles in the Driving series

The Official DSA Guide to Driving – the essential skills
The Official DSA Theory Test for Car Drivers
The Official DSA Theory Test for Car Drivers (CD-ROM)
Prepare for your Practical Driving Test (DVD)
DSA Driving Theory Quiz (DVD)

The Official DSA Guide to Riding – the essential skills
The Official DSA Theory Test for Motorcyclists
The Official DSA Theory Test for Motorcyclists (CD-ROM)
The Official DSA Guide to Learning to Ride
Better Biking – the Official DSA Training Aid (DVD)

The Official DSA Guide to Driving Buses and Coaches
The Official DSA Guide to Driving Goods Vehicles
The Official DSA Theory Test for Drivers of Large Vehicles
The Official DSA Theory Test for Drivers of Large Vehicles (CD-ROM)
Driver CPC – the Official DSA Guide for Professional Bus and Coach Drivers
Driver CPC – the Official DSA Guide for Professional Goods Vehicle Drivers

The Official DSA Guide to Tractor and Specialist Vehicle Driving Tests

The Official DSA Guide to Hazard Perception (DVD)
The Official Highway Code Interactive CD-ROM

75% recycled
This book is printed
on 75% recycled paper

Directgov

Directgov is the place to find all government motoring information and services. From logbooks to licensing, from driving tests to road tax, go to:

direct.gov.uk/motoring

Theory and practical tests
(Bookings and enquiries)

Online **direct.gov.uk/drivingtest**

Theory and practical tests

Enquiries and bookings **0300 200 1122**
Welsh speakers **0300 200 1133**

Practical tests
Minicom **0300 200 1144**
Fax **0300 200 1155**

Theory tests
Minicom **0300 200 1166**
Fax **0300 200 1177**
Customer Enquiry Unit **0300 200 1188**

DVA (Northern Ireland)
Theory test **0845 600 6700**
Practical test **0845 247 2471**

Driving Standards Agency
(Headquarters)

dft.gov.uk/dsa

The Axis Building,
112 Upper Parliament Street,
Nottingham NG1 6LP

Tel **0115 936 6666**
Fax **0115 936 6570**

Driver and Vehicle Agency (Testing) in Northern Ireland

dvani.gov.uk

Balmoral Road, Belfast BT12 6QL

Tel **02890 681 831**
Fax **02890 665 520**

Driver and Vehicle Licensing Agency
(GB licence enquiries)

dft.gov.uk/dvla

Longview Road, Swansea SA6 7JL

Tel **0300 790 6801**
Fax **0300 123 0798**
Minicom **0300 123 1278**

Driver and Vehicle Agency (Licensing) in Northern Ireland

dvani.gov.uk

County Hall, Castlerock Road,
Coleraine BT51 3TB

Tel **02870 341 469**
24 hour tel **0345 111 222**
Minicom **02870 341 380**

Office of the Parliamentary Commissioner for Administration

(The Parliamentary Ombudsman)

Millbank Tower, Millbank, London
SW1P 4QP

Tel **020 7217 4163**
Fax **020 7217 4160**

The Driving Standards Agency (DSA) is an executive agency of the Department for Transport. You'll see its logo at theory and practical test centres.

DSA aims to promote road safety through the advancement of driving standards, by

- establishing and developing high standards and best practice in driving and riding on the road; before people start to drive, as they learn, and after they pass their test
- ensuring high standards of instruction for different types of driver and rider
- conducting the statutory theory and practical tests efficiently, fairly and consistently across the country
- providing a centre of excellence for driver training and driving standards
- developing a range of publications and publicity material designed to promote safe driving for life.

The Driving Standards Agency recognises and values its customers. It will treat all its customers with respect, and deliver its services in an objective, polite and fair way.

dft.gov.uk/dsa

The Driver and Vehicle Agency (DVA) is an executive agency within the Department of the Environment for Northern Ireland.

Its primary aim is to promote and improve road safety through the advancement of driving standards and implementation of the Government's policies for improving the mechanical standards of vehicles.

dvani.gov.uk

Contents

04 The test and beyond

05 Other tests

Annexes

GETTING STARTED

This section covers
- Before you start
- Structured learning
- Your instructor
- Official study aids
- Practising
- Notes for the accompanying driver

A message from the Chief Driving Examiner

Being able to drive on your own opens up a whole new world of independence. It's important that before you apply for your practical test you are not only ready to pass, but are prepared for a lifetime of safe driving.

In this book we show the key skills you need to understand and master before taking your test. We refer to the *Driver's Record*; if you don't have one of these, ask your instructor for one, or you can download one from **direct.gov.uk/driversrecord**

You need to be capable of driving consistently, without help or prompting, to Level 5 in the *Driver's Record* before you take your practical test. Most people fail their test because they're not fully prepared, so make sure you have covered all the key skills to the standard we show in this book.

The key to gaining these skills is enough good tuition and plenty of practice. You should aim to gain experience driving in varying traffic conditions, on different types of road and under a wide range of differing weather conditions.

Trevor Wedge

Trevor Wedge
Chief Driving Examiner and
Director for Safer Driving

Before you start

First things first

You have decided you want to learn to drive. This will give you the opportunity to learn a completely new skill, one that will open up a whole new world of independence. But driving also comes with responsibility – it's important that you know how to drive safely and responsibly, that you learn the skills and that you practise. The aim is that you become a safe driver, not just to pass the test, but for life.

The first step is getting a provisional driving licence, but even before that you have to know that your eyesight is good enough to drive on the road.

Your eyesight

You can't drive on the road unless your eyesight meets certain requirements.

The easiest way to check this yourself is to try to read a number plate at the specified distance. If you can't, you should visit an optician before you start to drive.

The regulations state that, in good daylight, you should be able to read a vehicle number plate with letters 79.4 mm (3.1 inches) high at a minimum distance of 20.5 metres (about 67 feet). These are normally number plates in the older format (for example, X123XXX).

Number plates in the format (XX50XXX) have a narrower font and should be read from a distance of 20 metres (66 feet).

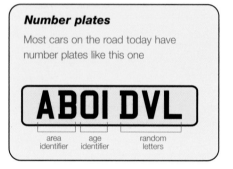

Number plates

Most cars on the road today have number plates like this one

ABOI DVL

area identifier   age identifier   random letters

If you need glasses or contact lenses to read the number plate, that's fine. However, you **MUST** wear them whenever you drive. If you have had sight correction surgery, you should declare this when you apply for your provisional licence.

You are responsible for ensuring that your eyesight meets the minimum legal requirements every time you drive. The police can stop you at any time and ask you to take an eyesight test. You'll also have to take one at the start of your practical test.

Applying for your licence

You must be at least 17 years old before you can get a provisional car licence. However, as an exception, if you receive Disability Living Allowance at the higher rate, you can get your provisional licence when you're 16.

Remember, you must have received your provisional driving licence before you start to drive on the road. This means that you must actually have it in your possession, not just have sent away for it.

Driving licences are issued by the Driver and Vehicle Licensing Agency (DVLA) and you can get an application form (D1) from any post office or online from **dft.gov.uk/dvla**.

In Northern Ireland the issuing authority is Driver and Vehicle Agency (Licensing) (DVA) and the form is a DL1 available online from **dvani.gov.uk**

Send your completed form to the appropriate office (details are given on the form). Remember to include a passport-type photograph as all provisional licences now issued are photocard licences.

When you receive your provisional licence, check that all the details are correct. If you need to contact DVLA or DVA, their telephone numbers are shown on page 3.

Structured learning

Learners who pass their driving test have had, on average, 45 hours of professional training combined with 22 hours of private practice. This shows the importance of combining professional training and private practice, while you are learning to drive.

To help you learn in a structured way, DSA has produced a *Driver's Record*.

The Driver's Record

The *Driver's Record* is a way of helping you and your driving instructor (see page 13) keep a record of your progress while you're learning to drive. You may have received one with your provisional licence. A copy of The *Driver's Record* can be downloaded – see page 13 for details of how to do this.

Following a structured learning programme, such as that contained in the *Driver's Record*, is beneficial to both you as a learner and your instructor. You need to learn the skill and then practise to get the experience.

You also need to learn both the theory and practical driving at the same time, especially now that the theory test contains a hazard perception part.

The record is a pocket-sized leaflet that you should take with you to all your driving lessons.

The *Driver's Record* contains a list of all the key skills which you need to achieve in order to pass your test and become a safe driver. It has space for your instructor to fill in as you progress through the various levels shown on the record.

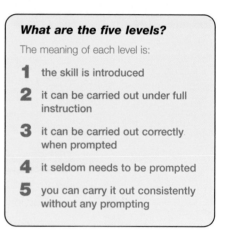

What are the five levels?

The meaning of each level is:

1 the skill is introduced

2 it can be carried out under full instruction

3 it can be carried out correctly when prompted

4 it seldom needs to be prompted

5 you can carry it out consistently without any prompting

Levels 1 to 4 should be initialled and dated by your instructor, and full details added when you reach **Level 5.** From this, you and your instructor will be able to see at a glance which topics you need to improve. Details of the 24 key skills can be found on pages 20-71 of this book. Section three gives corresponding advice for an accompanying driver.

The Driver's Record
will help to remind you what
you're trying to achieve,
how to get there and how
far you've got.

An important part of the structured learning process is practising what you have learnt during your lessons. Get together with your instructor and the person who will be helping you to practise, and discuss what you need to practise.

You can keep a record of any practice you have on different types of road and during different conditions between lessons on pages 148-151. Fill these in when you go out with the person helping you to practise. You can also record any worries you may have about your driving and then discuss these with your instructor (alternatively, printed sheets are available from your instructor).

You aren't ready to take your test until you have a complete set of signatures in the **Level 5** boxes. Only then can your instructor sign the declaration.

Where can I get hold of a Driver's Record?

If you haven't got one, ask your instructor, get one from your local driving test centre or download one by visiting **direct.gov.uk/driversrecord**.

By this time you should be able to drive safely without prompting. Don't forget to take the record with you when you go for your practical driving test.

Keep this as a record of your 'Learning to Drive' experience.

Your instructor

If you're going to pay someone to teach you to drive, they must be an Approved Driving Instructor (ADI) or hold a trainee licence.

DSA is responsible for checking the instructional standards of ADIs. All ADIs must

- have held a full driving licence for at least four years
- pass a challenging theory and practical test
- reach and keep up a high standard of instruction. ADIs are regularly checked by DSA
- be registered with DSA
- display a green ADI identification certificate on the windscreen of the tuition vehicle during lessons.

It's unlikely that anyone except an ADI would have the experience, knowledge and training to teach you properly.

Some trainee driving instructors are granted a trainee licence so that they can gain teaching experience before their qualifying examination. This licence is a pink identification certificate which must be displayed on the windscreen of the tuition vehicle during lessons.

Choosing an ADI

Ask friends or relatives for recommendations. Choose an instructor who has a good reputation, is reliable and punctual and whose car suits you. Ask the instructor for their grade before starting a course of lessons.

What does each instructor grade mean?

The standard of instruction of all ADIs is regularly checked by DSA. The instructor is then given a grade.

4 is satisfactory

5 is a good overall standard

6 is the highest

Remember, you can always ask to see the instructor's grade report.

Choosing the right instructor is vital to helping you develop as a driver. A good instructor will be happy to answer all your questions.

Ask if they have signed up to the industry Code of Practice. This is a voluntary code that covers the following

- their level of qualification
- the personal conduct expected from them when giving tuition
- the professional conduct of their business
- the acceptability of their advertising
- their method of dealing with complaints.

For further information or advice telephone DSA on **0300 200 1122** and choose 'instructor services' from the menu.

Take advice from your ADI – Your instructor will be able to help with all aspects of driving and advise you on

- what to study – DSA produce a range of books, CD-ROMs and DVDs to help you learn to drive
- how to practise and what you should be practising
- when you are ready for your test
- further training after you've passed your test (*Pass Plus* scheme – see page 126).

What if I find I don't like my instructor after I start lessons?

You can always find yourself a new instructor. It's important that you get on well with whoever is teaching you to drive. Different people prefer different teaching styles. You should try to find someone that suits you.

Can I have lessons in my own car?

Some instructors are prepared to give lessons in your own car, if you are lucky enough to have one. Ask about this when you first contact them as some instructors will not do so for health and safety reasons.

Official study aids

Lessons and practice are the most important elements of learning to drive, but there is something you can do when you're not in the car. There are various books and electronic products to help you with all stages of driving – theory, hazard perception and practical.

The Official Highway Code – Contains all the up-to-date rules and regulations about using the roads. It's essential reading for everyone – buy a copy of the latest edition, as it will be a most useful reference book. *The Highway Code* is also available as an interactive CD-ROM or in British Sign Language.

DSA also produces a series of books and electronic products to provide you with a sound knowledge of driving skills.

The Official DSA Theory Test for Car Drivers – Includes all the questions and answers in the multiple choice part of the theory test and explains why all the answers are correct. It contains lots of useful information and now also includes *The Official Highway Code*. The questions are regularly updated, so make sure that you have the latest version. If you're well prepared you won't find the questions difficult.

This information is also produced in CD-ROM format for those who prefer an interactive way of learning. In this format you can take as many mock tests as you like before you actually take your real test.

The Official DSA Guide to Hazard Perception DVD – Is an interactive DVD to help you prepare for the hazard perception parts of the theory and practical tests.

All the official training materials listed are available online at **tsoshop.co.uk/dsa** or by mail order from **0870 241 4523**.

They are also available from bookshops and selected computer software retailers.

It has clear guidance on how to recognise and respond to hazards and is packed with useful tips, quizzes and expert advice. It also includes interactive hazard perception clips and your performance will receive a score so you'll know if you're ready to pass.

The CD-ROM and DVD are available individually or packaged together as *The Official DSA Complete Theory Test Kit* which provides all the learning materials for the theory test in one package.

The Official DSA Guide to Driving - the essential skills – This book is referenced in Section two (key skills). It contains a wealth of information about driving skills, from the basic, helping you when you first start to drive, through to in-depth advice about dealing with various road and traffic conditions.

Prepare for your Practical Driving Test DVD – This DVD (formerly called *The Official DSA Guide to Learning to Drive DVD*) has been produced to accompany this book. It's presented in a very lively and animated way. It shows the standard at which you need to drive to reach **Level 5** in the *Driver's Record*.

This interactive DVD helps you to understand what is needed to reach the standard and gives you many hints and tips on becoming a safe driver. It also shows how the examiner conducts the practical driving test, taking you through various parts of the test.

Practising

As stated earlier, those who pass their driving test have had, on average, 45 hours of professional training combined with 22 hours of private practice. This is the average, but generally the more driving experience you get, the better. You need to gain experience on all different types of road and driving conditions. The more you practise and increase your experience, the more confident you will become.

Your accompanying driver

The person helping you to practise must be at least 21 years old and have held a full EC/EEA licence for that type of car (automatic or manual) for at least the last three years. (Your accompanying driver cannot ask for payment for helping you practise.)

The practice vehicle

The vehicle in which you practise must be roadworthy and properly insured for you to drive. If you drive while uninsured you will be committing a serious offence. The vehicle must also display L plates (or D plates in Wales) to the front and rear – make sure they are secure and don't obstruct your view.

Get together with both your instructor and the person who will be helping you to practise so you can discuss what you need to do. Ask your instructor for advice on what skills you should practise after each lesson.

How to practise

You should vary what you do. Try to practise

- on as many types of road as you can
- in all sorts of traffic and weather conditions, even in the dark
- on dual carriageways where the national speed limit applies. You may be asked to drive on this type of road during the test.

As you practise in these different conditions and on different types of road, log your hours and miles on pages 148-151. This will help you to remember and quantify the amount of practice you have had in the different conditions. When you practise, try to

- avoid obstructing other traffic. Most drivers are tolerant of learners, but don't try their patience too much
- consider the local residents. For example, don't repeatedly practise emergency stops in the same quiet residential streets or practise on test routes
- get lots of general driving. Don't just concentrate on the exercises included in the practical test.

There are more helpful suggestions for the person accompanying you in Section three of this book.

Notes for the accompanying driver

Agreeing to accompany a learner is a responsibility not to be taken lightly. You will be the person helping your learner get that important extra practice.

Your help won't replace good professional tuition but it will enable your learner to get experience while driving in different conditions.

You must make sure that you have the right licence and that your car is insured for them to drive (see previous page). You will also need L plates (D plates in Wales) and an additional interior mirror so that you can check what's happening behind.

When you accompany a learner you're responsible for their actions. You'll need to stay calm and offer advice when needed. Have a chat with your learner and their instructor so that together you can decide what needs to be practised. Remember also that you **MUST NOT** use a mobile phone or other hand-held device while the provisional licence holder is driving a motor vehicle on a road.

As the full licence holder, you are still responsible for the vehicle while supervising the learner. You **CANNOT** concentrate fully, watch out for danger, or guide their actions safely while you are distracted with a phone conversation. You are breaking the law if you use your mobile while your learner is driving. **Don't take the chance.**

Everyone learns at a different pace and finds different things difficult. Something that you find easy may be difficult for a learner. Be patient and constructive. Make sure you're aware of the standard that is expected of a learner driver and the style of driving they are being taught. Some things may have changed since you learnt to drive and it can be confusing for the learner to receive different messages.

Remember, you can't receive payment for the time you spend helping your learner to practise.

Section three of this book contains lots of further advice, aimed at the accompanying driver, which covers all of the 24 key skills in addition to general hints and tips. Record your time spent in different situations on pages 148-151. This gives a permanent record of time spent and miles travelled and will help the three of you work out where extra practice would be useful.

section **two**
KEY SKILLS

This section covers

- Using this book
- Legal responsibilities
- Cockpit checks
- Safety checks
- Controls and instruments
- Moving away and stopping
- Safe positioning
- Mirrors – vision and use
- Signals
- Anticipation and planning
- Use of speed
- Other traffic
- Junctions
- Roundabouts
- Dual carriageways
- Pedestrian crossings
- Turning the vehicle around
- Reversing
- Parking
- Emergency stop
- Independent driving
- Darkness
- Weather conditions
- Environmental issues
- Passengers and loads
- Security

Using this book

Use this book as a reference while you are learning to drive. It can also be used to keep a record of your progress.

Reaching Level 5

All the key skills from the *Driver's Record* are shown on the following pages. On these pages you'll find details about what standard you need to reach to become a safe driver in that skill and achieve a **Level 5** marking in your *Driver's Record*.

As your instructor signs off the skill in your *Driver's Record*, make a note on the relevant page in this book.

Expert tips

As well as explaining the level that you need to achieve, there are also useful tips from the people who set the tests. These have been drawn up from years of experience and from common mistakes made by candidates during their driving tests.

Recap questions

For each skill there are recap questions – try answering these to refresh your memory.

All the answers to the recap questions can be found in the books referred to at the foot of the relevant pages.

What to expect on test

Once you have reached **Level 5** in all the key skills and are ready to take your test, there's some useful information about what to expect on the test and what the examiner will be looking for.

How do I use the references?

Further information about each of the skills can be found by following the references at the foot of the relevant pages. The reference **HC** refers to *The Official Highway Code* and the reference **DES** refers to *The Official DSA Guide to Driving – the essential skills*.

The **HC** references are prefixed with either the letter **r** or **p**. The letter **r** indicates the rule number and the letter **p** indicates the page number.

The **DES** references are prefixed with the letter **s** and this indicates the section of the book.

See the example below.

| **References** | **HC** r245, p35 | **DES** s2 |

Legal responsibilities

As a driver it is your responsibility to know how the law relates to both yourself and your vehicle, so make sure you're up to date with the rules and regulations.

You need to comply with the **rules and regulations:**

LEVEL 5 — You are in a fit condition to drive safely

To do this you need to understand how the following affects you...

- **health** – certain medical conditions must be reported to DVLA

- **eyesight** – can you read a number plate as shown on page 10. If you need glasses to read it clearly then you must always wear them when you're driving

- **drink** – don't drink and drive. There's a legal limit but it's safer not to drink at all if you're going to drive

- **drugs** – never take drugs before driving, the effect can be more severe than alcohol. Even some prescription drugs can make you drowsy

- **tiredness** – if you're tired you're more likely to have an accident. On a long journey have a break every two hours or so

- **mobile phones** – it's illegal to use a hand-held phone while driving and even hands-free can distract you from your driving.

LEVEL 5 — You and the car you're driving comply with the regulations

To do this you must ensure that...

- the vehicle is taxed and has a valid MOT certificate if it's more than three years old

- the vehicle is insured for you to drive

- the vehicle is in a roadworthy condition

- your driving licence is in order.

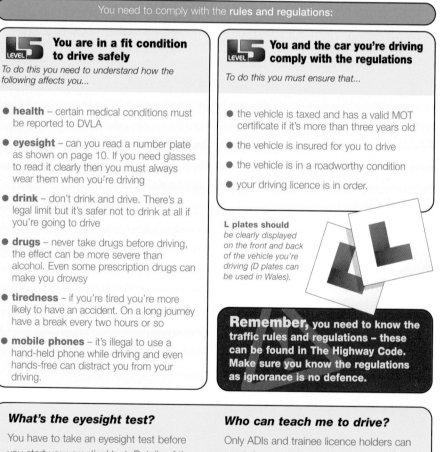

L plates should *be clearly displayed on the front and back of the vehicle you're driving (D plates can be used in Wales).*

Remember, you need to know the traffic rules and regulations – these can be found in The Highway Code. Make sure you know the regulations as ignorance is no defence.

What's the eyesight test?

You have to take an eyesight test before you start your practical test. Details of the requirements are given on page 10.

Who can teach me to drive?

Only ADIs and trainee licence holders can teach for payment. They must display a badge on the windscreen during lessons.

Tips from the experts

Make sure you know what to do if you are involved in a road traffic incident. Keep calm and, as well as dealing with the scene of the incident, you may need to report it to the police.

Even hands-free phones distract you from your driving so it's safer not to use one at all. Switch your phone off otherwise you might be tempted to answer it if it rings. Stop safely to retrieve any messages.

The regulations about mobile phones also apply to the person accompanying you as you practise.

What to expect on test

You'll be asked about legal responsibilities during your theory test. You'll need to show the relevant papers and pass the eyesight check before starting your practical test.

Recap questions

Q1 *What are the legal requirements for someone helping a learner to drive?*

Q2 *What's the first thing you should do if you are involved in a road traffic incident?*

Accompanying driver advice | p84

Keep a record

Notes

Your instructor should keep a record of your progress on your *Driver's Record*. You may also like to fill in your progress below and make any notes that might help you in this space:

1	**3**	**5**
introduced	prompted	independent
		dd/mm/yy

References | **HC** most of the Code | **DES** s2

Cockpit checks

These checks may be simple, but they are essential. The car you are using needs to be comfortable and ready for you to drive before you turn the key in the ignition.

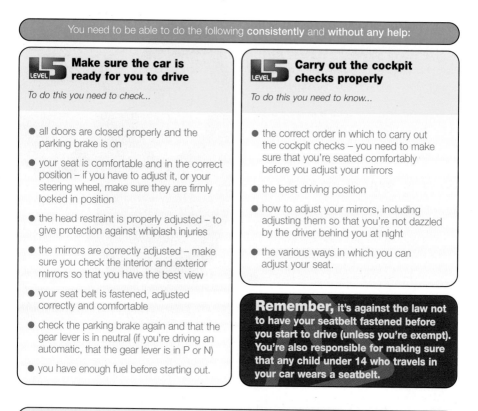

You need to be able to do the following **consistently** and **without any help:**

LEVEL 5 — Make sure the car is ready for you to drive

To do this you need to check...

- all doors are closed properly and the parking brake is on

- your seat is comfortable and in the correct position – if you have to adjust it, or your steering wheel, make sure they are firmly locked in position

- the head restraint is properly adjusted – to give protection against whiplash injuries

- the mirrors are correctly adjusted – make sure you check the interior and exterior mirrors so that you have the best view

- your seat belt is fastened, adjusted correctly and comfortable

- check the parking brake again and that the gear lever is in neutral (if you're driving an automatic, that the gear lever is in P or N)

- you have enough fuel before starting out.

LEVEL 5 — Carry out the cockpit checks properly

To do this you need to know...

- the correct order in which to carry out the cockpit checks – you need to make sure that you're seated comfortably before you adjust your mirrors

- the best driving position

- how to adjust your mirrors, including adjusting them so that you're not dazzled by the driver behind you at night

- the various ways in which you can adjust your seat.

Remember, it's against the law not to have your seatbelt fastened before you start to drive (unless you're exempt). You're also responsible for making sure that any child under 14 who travels in your car wears a seatbelt.

Can I adjust the mirrors while I'm driving?

Never try to do this on the move – if you need to readjust your mirrors or seat position, find a safe place to stop first.

Do I need to do these checks every time?

Get into the habit of doing these checks every time – it's particularly important if other people use the car.

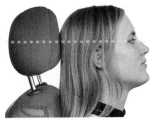

The rigid part of the restraint should support the back of your head.

Fasten your seatbelt every time – it's against the law not to do so.

Make sure the gear lever is in neutral before starting the engine.

Tips from the experts

Make sure you do these checks, in the right order, before you start the engine. This is particularly important if you are not the only person using the car.

What to expect on test

Your examiner will watch to make sure that you carry out all the checks, in the right order, before you start the engine.

Recap questions

Q1 Is it the responsibility of the driver to make sure that adult passengers wear seatbelts?

Q2 What could be a consequence of failing to carry out the cockpit checks properly?

Q3 Why should you check that the head restraint is in the correct position?

Accompanying driver advice   p85

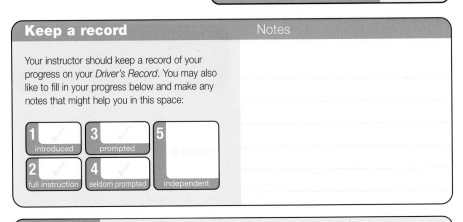

Keep a record

Your instructor should keep a record of your progress on your *Driver's Record*. You may also like to fill in your progress below and make any notes that might help you in this space:

1 ✓ introduced
2 ✓ full instruction
3 ✓ prompted
4 ✓ seldom prompted
5 independent

Notes

References   **HC** r97, 99   **DES** s3-5

Safety checks

It's important that your car is in good working order before you start the engine. You need to be aware of what to check, how to do it and how often to do it.

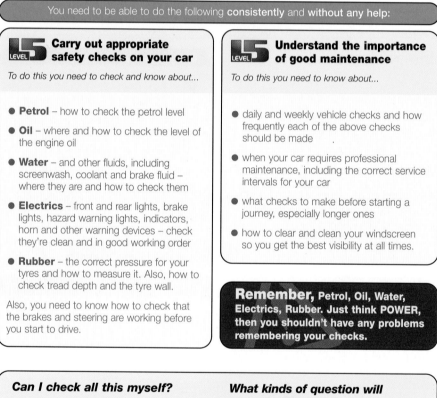

You need to be able to do the following **consistently** and **without any help:**

LEVEL 5 — Carry out appropriate safety checks on your car

To do this you need to check and know about...

- **Petrol** – how to check the petrol level
- **Oil** – where and how to check the level of the engine oil
- **Water** – and other fluids, including screenwash, coolant and brake fluid – where they are and how to check them
- **Electrics** – front and rear lights, brake lights, hazard warning lights, indicators, horn and other warning devices – check they're clean and in good working order
- **Rubber** – the correct pressure for your tyres and how to measure it. Also, how to check tread depth and the tyre wall.

Also, you need to know how to check that the brakes and steering are working before you start to drive.

LEVEL 5 — Understand the importance of good maintenance

To do this you need to know about...

- daily and weekly vehicle checks and how frequently each of the above checks should be made
- when your car requires professional maintenance, including the correct service intervals for your car
- what checks to make before starting a journey, especially longer ones
- how to clear and clean your windscreen so you get the best visibility at all times.

Remember, Petrol, Oil, Water, Electrics, Rubber. Just think POWER, then you shouldn't have any problems remembering your checks.

Can I check all this myself?

You'll need to get someone to help you check the brake lights. It's also easier and quicker to check the other lights if you can get someone to look while you are working the controls.

What kinds of question will I be asked on test?

There is only a limited number of safety check questions that you can be asked on test. They can all be found online at **direct.gov.uk/motoring**

Tips from the experts

Make sure that you're familiar with the car you're driving, and that you can explain or demonstrate how you would carry out simple safety checks on that car.

You will need to open the bonnet to carry out some of the checks – make sure you know how to open the bonnet and also that you shut it properly once you've carried out the checks.

Regular servicing will keep the engine more efficient and save you money in the long run.

What to expect on test

At the start of the test your examiner will ask you to

- explain how you would carry out certain safety checks
- demonstrate how you would carry out certain safety checks.

Recap question

Q1 *What's the minimum tread depth for your car tyres?*

Accompanying driver advice   **p86**

Keep a record   Notes

Your instructor should keep a record of your progress on your *Driver's Record*. You may also like to fill in your progress below and make any notes that might help you in this space:

| **1** introduced | **3** prompted | **5** |
| **2** full instruction | **4** seldom prompted | independent |

References   **HC** r89, 97, p128   **DES** s5, 14

Controls and instruments

You need to concentrate on what's happening around you when you're driving, so operating the vehicle's controls should be second nature.

You need to be able to do the following **consistently** and **without any help**:

LEVEL 5 Operate the controls safely without looking

To do this you need to be able to use the following controls correctly...

- **foot controls** – the accelerator, clutch and footbrake pedals

- **hand controls** – the parking brake, steering wheel, indicators, headlights and gearstick

- **other controls** – the horn (you need to know when and for what reason you can legally use the horn), windscreen wipers, demister and heated windows. You also need to be aware of any controls specific to the car you are driving.

Remember, you need to be aware of the consequences of what happens if you use the controls incorrectly.

LEVEL 5 Read the various instruments of the car you're driving

To do this you need to know...

- the meaning and function of each element of the instrument panel including the warning lights and speedometer.

Your speedometer
must show miles per hour and kilometres per hour.

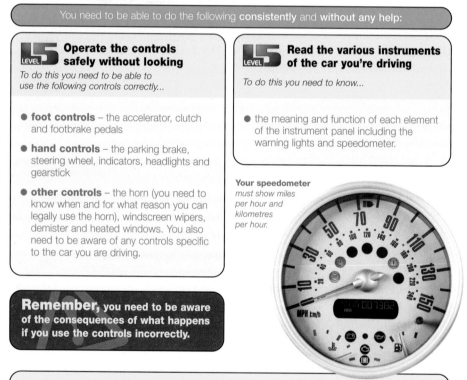

Can I look at the gear lever?

If the car is moving you shouldn't take your eyes off the road to look at the gear lever. You should already know what gear you're in. Don't coast with the gear lever in neutral or the clutch pedal down.

Should I steer and change gear at the same time?

You need both hands to steer. Try to change to the appropriate gear and then ensure both hands are on the wheel before starting to turn the steering wheel.

Tips from the experts

Balance your use of the accelerator and clutch so that you pull away smoothly and then accelerate gradually to gain speed. Don't accelerate fiercely or use the clutch sharply.

If you're driving an automatic car, make sure you understand the procedure fully.

Brake smoothly and in good time and don't apply the parking brake until the car has stopped. Make sure you don't try to move off with the parking brake on.

Choose the right gear for your speed and the road conditions and ensure that you're in the correct gear to deal with any hazard or junction safely.

Keep your steering steady and smooth.

What to expect on test

Your examiner will want to see that you can

- demonstrate good control of the vehicle throughout the test
- show an understanding of the vehicle's instruments.

Recap question

Q1 *When is it illegal to use your horn?*

Accompanying driver advice   p87

Keep a record

Notes

Your instructor should keep a record of your progress on your *Driver's Record*. You may also like to fill in your progress below and make any notes that might help you in this space:

| 1 ✓ introduced | 3 ✓ prompted | 5 independent |
| 2 ✓ full instruction | 4 ✓ seldom prompted | |

References   HC r110   DES s3

Moving away and stopping

You have to move away and stop every time you drive and that's why it's so important to make sure that you know the correct way to move away and stop safely.

You need to be able to do the following **consistently** and **without any help:**

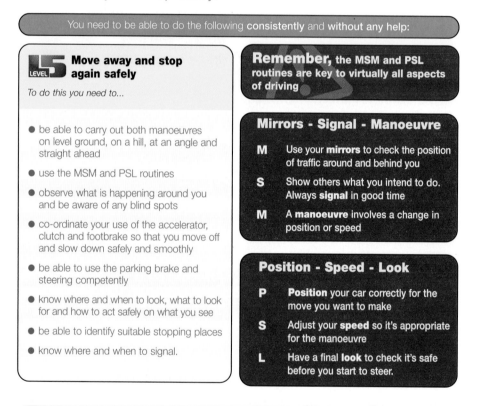

LEVEL 5 Move away and stop again safely

To do this you need to...

- be able to carry out both manoeuvres on level ground, on a hill, at an angle and straight ahead
- use the MSM and PSL routines
- observe what is happening around you and be aware of any blind spots
- co-ordinate your use of the accelerator, clutch and footbrake so that you move off and slow down safely and smoothly
- be able to use the parking brake and steering competently
- know where and when to look, what to look for and how to act safely on what you see
- be able to identify suitable stopping places
- know where and when to signal.

Remember, the MSM and PSL routines are key to virtually all aspects of driving

Mirrors - Signal - Manoeuvre

M   Use your **mirrors** to check the position of traffic around and behind you

S   Show others what you intend to do. Always **signal** in good time

M   A **manoeuvre** involves a change in position or speed

Position - Speed - Look

P   **Position** your car correctly for the move you want to make

S   Adjust your **speed** so it's appropriate for the manoeuvre

L   Have a final **look** to check it's safe before you start to steer.

What if I don't have a clear view of the road?

If you can't see because someone has parked close to you, edge out slowly and only move off when you can see it's safe.

How do I stop if someone is following very closely?

Make sure you signal in good time to let them know that you're going to slow down and stop.

You may need to check your blind spot more than once when moving off from behind another car.

Tips from the experts

Always use your mirrors but only signal if you need to – don't just signal automatically.

Check your blind spots. Don't pull out without looking or make anyone else stop or swerve.

Move off smoothly in the correct gear and don't accelerate excessively.

What to expect on test

Your examiner may ask you to stop at the side of the road and then move away again. Every time you perform either of these manoeuvres the examiner will watch your

- use of the controls and MSM routine each time you move off and stop – don't forget to incorporate the PSL routine when stopping

- observation of, and safe responses to, other road users

- judgement in selecting a safe and suitable place to stop.

Recap questions

Q1 *When would you not need to signal before moving away?*

Q2 *What are you looking for in a safe place to stop?*

Accompanying driver advice p88

Keep a record

Your instructor should keep a record of your progress on your *Driver's Record*. You may also like to fill in your progress below and make any notes that might help you in this space:

| 1 ✓ introduced | 3 ✓ prompted | 5 independent |
| 2 ✓ full instruction | 4 ✓ seldom prompted | |

Notes

References **HC** r103, 159-161, 238-252   **DES** s5

Safe positioning

Make sure you drive in the correct position for the road on which you're travelling. It's not only important for your safety but also for the safety of other road users.

You need to be able to do the following **consistently** and **without any help**:

LEVEL 5 Keep a safe position during normal driving

To do this you should be able to...

- use the MSM and PSL routines (see page 30)
- follow the principles of lane discipline. Plan ahead and make sure you move into the correct lane in good time
- show an understanding of how a wide or narrow road would affect the position you would choose
- keep a safe position during normal driving, especially around bends
- take up the correct position on a one-way street.

LEVEL 5 Respond to the positions of other road users

To do this you must understand...

- how other vehicles, such as lorries and cyclists, need to position themselves
- what clearance you need to leave when passing stationary vehicles or obstructions.

Remember, plan ahead and make sure you move into the correct lane in good time. Don't change lanes at the last minute.

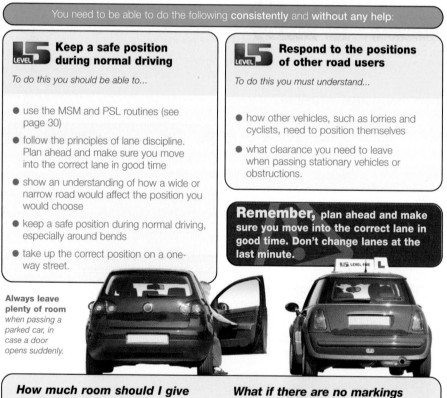

Always leave plenty of room *when passing a parked car, in case a door opens suddenly.*

How much room should I give a cyclist when overtaking?

Give them plenty of room, as much room as you would give a car. They may have to move away from the kerb in order to avoid something you can't see.

What if there are no markings on the road?

Position your vehicle sensibly even if there are no road markings. Don't drive too close to the kerb or too close to the centre of the road.

Tips from the experts

Don't obstruct other road users by being in the wrong lane, straddling lanes or weaving in and out.

At roundabouts, make sure you don't cut across the path of other vehicles.

Make sure everyone around you knows where you want to go.

Follow the road markings and get into the correct lane as soon as possible.

What to expect on test

Your examiner will watch to make sure that you

- are using the MSM and PSL routines and acting on what you have seen
- respond to signs and road markings by selecting the correct lane in good time
- keep a safe position for the situation.

Recap questions

Q1 When should you use the right-hand lane of a dual carriageway?

Q2 A large vehicle is emerging from a junction on the right. How might this affect your positioning?

Q3 Why is it important to move into the correct lane as soon as you can?

Accompanying driver advice   p89

Keep a record

Notes

Your instructor should keep a record of your progress on your *Driver's Record*. You may also like to fill in your progress below and make any notes that might help you in this space:

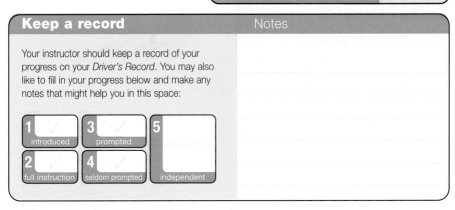

1 ✓	3 ✓	5
introduced	prompted	
2 ✓	4 ✓	
full instruction	seldom prompted	independent

References   **HC** r127-146, 152-156   **DES** s7, 8

Mirrors – vision and use

Effective and well-timed observation should form part of your driving routine. You must know what's happening around you at all times and act safely on what you see.

> You need to be able to do the following **consistently** and **without any help**:

LEVEL 5 — Effective use of all the mirrors at all times

To do this you must know...

- how to make use of the MSM and PSL routines (see page 30)
- when to use the mirrors and how often to use them
- why you need to use the mirrors and the importance of regular updates
- how to act on what you see in your mirrors.

LEVEL 5 — Show knowledge of how the mirrors differ

To do this you need to know...

- the uses for the interior mirror and the two exterior mirrors
- the effect that flat, concave and convex mirrors have on how you interpret what you see in them
- what areas each mirror covers and where the blind spots are.

Remember, there are blind spots between what you can see when looking forward and what you can see in your mirrors. The car's bodywork also creates blind spots which can hide smaller road users. This picture highlights where these areas are.

How do I check my blind spots when I'm moving?

It's dangerous to look over your shoulder as you may lose touch with what is happening in front, but you can give a quick sideways glance.

Which mirror should I look in first?

Normally you should look in the interior mirror first followed by both exterior mirrors. You need to check that no one is attempting to move up on either side.

Tips from the experts

Always look before you signal, look and signal before you act and then act sensibly on what you see – just looking isn't enough to keep you safe.

Use all of your mirrors periodically while you drive, especially as you approach any hazard, so that you're constantly aware of what is happening around you.

Never manoeuvre before looking in your mirrors. Make sure that you always use your mirrors before

- moving off
- signalling
- turning left or right
- changing lanes or overtaking
- changing speed or stopping
- opening your car door.

What to expect on test

Your examiner will watch to make sure you're aware of the scene all around, so you need to make sure that you use all your mirrors and act safely on what you see.

Recap question

Q1 *What are the advantages and disadvantages of convex mirrors?*

Accompanying driver advice | p89

Keep a record

Notes

Your instructor should keep a record of your progress on your *Driver's Record*. You may also like to fill in your progress below and make any notes that might help you in this space:

1 ✓ introduced	**3** ✓ prompted	**5**
2 ✓ full instruction	**4** ✓ seldom prompted	independent

References | **HC** r161 | **DES** s4

Signals

You need to understand, and respond safely to, signals given by other motorists and give clear, well-timed signals to other road users so that they know what you're planning to do.

You need to be able to do the following **consistently** and **without any help**:

LEVEL 5 — Give correct signals
To do this you need to know...

- why it is necessary to give signals – you need to signal to let others know what you intend to do

- when and how to give signals (it's important that you time your signal to allow others to respond safely)

- when and how to give arm signals

- when signals are not required.

LEVEL 5 — Read others' signals
To do this you need to know...

- the significance of other types of signals including brake, reversing and hazard warning lights

- how to read signals given by traffic controllers such as the police.

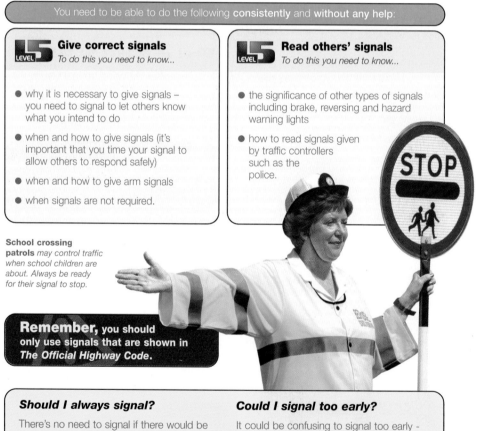

School crossing patrols *may control traffic when school children are about. Always be ready for their signal to stop.*

Remember, you should only use signals that are shown in *The Official Highway Code.*

Should I always signal?

There's no need to signal if there would be no benefit to other road users. If you have a clear view and can see that no one else is around, there's no reason to signal.

Could I signal too early?

It could be confusing to signal too early - for example, if there are several side roads close together. Think about the situation before you give a signal.

1 Fog light

In seriously reduced visibility fog lights can help to make vehicles easier to see

2 Reversing light

Shows a vehicle is about to reverse or reversing. When you're reversing it helps you to see what is behind you in the dark

3 Indicator light

Indicators normally show a change of direction. Both indicators flashing may mean a vehicle is stopped ahead

4 Rear/brake light

Brake lights can often be an early warning of what's happening further down the road

Tips from the experts

Don't be tempted to flash your headlights for any other reason than that shown in *The Official Highway Code*.

Always make sure to cancel your signal after you have carried out a manoeuvre. Leaving a signal on can lead to dangerous situations because other road users may take action based on the direction they expect you to take.

What to expect on test

The examiner will expect well-timed signals and safe responses to signals from others.

Recap questions

Q1 *When can you flash your headlights?*

Q2 *In what kind of a situation would you not have to signal?*

Accompanying driver advice   **p91**

Keep a record   Notes

Your instructor should keep a record of your progress on your *Driver's Record*. You may also like to fill in your progress below and make any notes that might help you in this space:

1 introduced	3 prompted	5
2 full instruction	4 seldom prompted	independent

References   **HC** r103-112, 116, p102   **DES** s5, 10

Anticipation and planning

These skills are found in all areas of driving. You should always be aware of what is going on around you while planning what you need to do in response.

> You need to be able to do the following **consistently** and **without any help**:

LEVEL 5 Plan ahead to respond safely to others' actions

To do this you need to be able to...

- use the MSM and PSL routines (see page 30)
- identify hazards from clues and respond to them safely
- recognise times, places and conditions which mean there is a higher risk. This includes weather conditions
- use scanning techniques to enable you to plan ahead so that you can prioritise how you will deal with hazards you encounter.

Remember, you'll need to plan ahead to deal with static hazards like traffic lights and road works.

LEVEL 5 Anticipate the actions of all types of road users

To do this you need to be familiar with the risks associated with each type of road user...

- **cyclists** – take special care when you cross cycle lanes and watch out for cyclists passing on your left
- **motorcyclists** – look for them, especially at junctions and in slow-moving traffic
- **pedestrians** – take special care with the very young, older people and those with disabilities. They may not have seen you and could step out suddenly
- **animals** – give horse riders as much room as possible and pass them slowly
- **emergency vehicles** – don't panic, check where they're coming from and try to keep out of their way. If necessary, pull into the side of the road and stop.

Can I use my hazard warning lights while I am moving?

Yes, you can use them to warn other drivers of a hazard or an obstruction ahead, but only on a motorway or unrestricted dual carriageway (on all other roads you must be stationary).

What do I gain from anticipating and planning?

If you scan ahead you should be able to anticipate potentially hazardous situations. By being prepared, you minimise the element of surprise, leaving you to deal with situations safely in a controlled way.

Tips from the experts

You need to be constantly checking what's going on behind and around you. Planning ahead means that you won't find yourself in a situation where you have to stop suddenly.

Take every opportunity to look for clues like reflections in windows or feet under a van which might tell you what is going to happen next. Even when you're stationary the scene is constantly changing.

What to expect on test

You will be expected to be aware of other road users and road and weather conditions at all times. You will also need to show an awareness of the hazards they present and respond safely in good time.

Recap questions

Q1 *What hazards could you come across on a busy residential street?*

Q2 *Why might a motorcyclist need to swerve suddenly?*

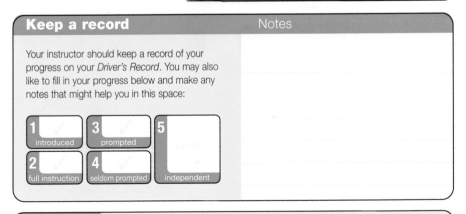

If a cyclist looks over their shoulder, *hold back, they may be about to cross your path.*

Accompanying driver advice   p92

Keep a record

Your instructor should keep a record of your progress on your *Driver's Record*. You may also like to fill in your progress below and make any notes that might help you in this space:

1 introduced
2 full instruction
3 prompted
4 seldom prompted
5 independent

Notes

References   **HC** r146, 160-161, 204-237   **DES** s7, 10

Use of speed

Your speed should be based on various factors including the condition of the road, weather and traffic, and the presence of pedestrians. Always drive within the speed limit.

You need to be able to do the following **consistently** and **without any help**:

 Drive at an appropriate speed for the conditions

To do this you need to know...

- national speed limits and restrictions for different types of road and any restricted speed limits for the road you're on

- the appropriate speed for particular road, weather and traffic conditions

- the appropriate speed to use where there are pedestrians and in traffic-calmed areas

- the stopping distance for your vehicle in different conditions and how to calculate a safe separation distance between yourself and the vehicle in front.

Remember, speed limits don't mean that you have to travel at that speed. Use your judgement and drive according to the conditions.

Never break the speed limit – *speed cameras are only there to make sure everyone is driving within the speed limits.*

Can I exceed the speed limit to overtake someone?

No, you must always stay within the speed limit. It is illegal to break it, even for a short period of time. Driving faster is dangerous and remember, speed kills.

Can I drive too slowly?

You should drive confidently and at a reasonable speed. If you drive too slowly or hesitate unnecessarily it can be very frustrating for other drivers and can lead to road traffic incidents.

Tips from the experts

Don't drive too fast for the road and traffic conditions and make sure that you can stop safely, well within the distance you can see to be clear. Leave extra distance for stopping on wet or slippery roads.

Don't change your speed unpredictably.

Don't approach junctions too fast, or too slowly. Avoid being over-cautious or stopping and waiting when it's safe to go.

What to expect on test

Your examiner will watch how you control your speed throughout the drive and will want to see that you can

- make reasonable progress along the road and respond to changing conditions
- keep up with other traffic but comply with the speed limits
- show confidence together with sound judgement.

Recap questions

Q1 *What's the national speed limit for cars on a dual carriageway?*

Q2 *What separation distance should you leave between you and the vehicle in front on a wet road?*

Accompanying driver advice   p93

Keep a record

Notes

Your instructor should keep a record of your progress on your *Driver's Record*. You may also like to fill in your progress below and make any notes that might help you in this space:

1 ✓ introduced	3 ✓ prompted	5 independent
2 ✓ full instruction	4 ✓ seldom prompted	

References   **HC** r124-126, p42-43   **DES** s7, 10

41

Other traffic

In most cases when you're driving there will be other traffic on the road. You need to be able to deal safely and confidently when meeting, crossing and overtaking other vehicles.

> You need to be able to do the following **consistently** and **without any help:**

 Safely negotiate situations involving other traffic

To do this you need to be confident when dealing with these situations...

- **meeting** – where there are parked cars or obstructions on your side of the road you must be prepared to give way to oncoming traffic. On narrow roads you may need to use passing places

- **crossing** – you normally need to cross the path of other traffic if you're turning right into a side road or driveway. Make sure you position your car correctly, as close to the centre of the road as is safe and watch out for oncoming traffic, stopping if necessary. Don't cut the corner or take the turn too widely

- **overtaking** – overtake only if you can do so legally and safely. Check the speed and position of any vehicles behind (they might be planning to overtake you), in front, and coming towards you before you decide to overtake.

Understand the rules for dealing with these situations

To do this you need to be aware of...

- the MSM and PSL routines (see page 30)

- why and when to give way – you shouldn't cause another road user to slow down or alter their course when they have priority

- the significance of passing places, warning signs, road markings and how to deal with obstructions

- the importance of planning and anticipation and acting safely on what you see

- how to drive on all road types – a one-way or two-way road (including a three-lane two-way), a major or minor road, a narrow road or a dual carriageway.

Remember, pedestrians have priority if they're crossing the road into which you are turning.

If a driver is indicating, can I pull out before they turn?

Always wait until you are sure they are turning before you move out. They may have forgotten to cancel their signal.

Can I flash my lights to give someone the go ahead?

No. *The Official Highway Code* states that you should only flash your lights to let someone know you are there as a warning.

Tips from the experts

When passing parked cars, watch out for doors opening, pedestrians (especially children) stepping out from between the cars or vehicles pulling out.

When overtaking cyclists or horse riders, slow right down and give them as much room as you would a car.

If you're going to pass an obstruction or overtake, start planning early so that you get a better view of the road ahead.

What to expect on test

Your examiner will watch to see how you

- apply the MSM and PSL routines
- respond to road and traffic conditions
- handle the car's controls.

If there's an obstruction on your side of the road, plan ahead so that you can give way to oncoming traffic.

Recap questions

Q1 *Give three examples of where it is against the law to overtake*

Q2 *On which side can you pass traffic, when on a one-way road?*

Q3 *You see a car coming towards you on a narrow road. There is a passing place just ahead on the other side of the road. What should you do?*

Accompanying driver advice | p95

Keep a record

Notes

Your instructor should keep a record of your progress on your *Driver's Record*. You may also like to fill in your progress below and make any notes that might help you in this space:

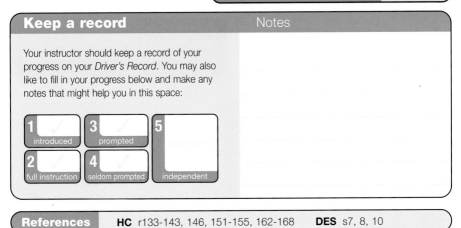

1 introduced
2 full instruction
3 prompted
4 seldom prompted
5 independent

References | HC r133-143, 146, 151-155, 162-168 **DES** s7, 8, 10

Junctions

There are many different types of junction. You need to be able to negotiate any junction on any type of road safely without holding up other traffic unnecessarily.

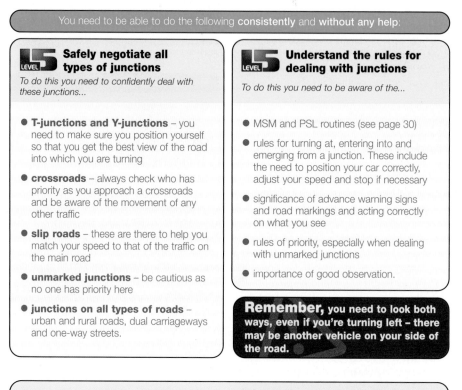

You need to be able to do the following **consistently** and **without any help**:

LEVEL 5 Safely negotiate all types of junctions

To do this you need to confidently deal with these junctions...

- **T-junctions and Y-junctions** – you need to make sure you position yourself so that you get the best view of the road into which you are turning

- **crossroads** – always check who has priority as you approach a crossroads and be aware of the movement of any other traffic

- **slip roads** – these are there to help you match your speed to that of the traffic on the main road

- **unmarked junctions** – be cautious as no one has priority here

- **junctions on all types of roads** – urban and rural roads, dual carriageways and one-way streets.

LEVEL 5 Understand the rules for dealing with junctions

To do this you need to be aware of the...

- MSM and PSL routines (see page 30)

- rules for turning at, entering into and emerging from a junction. These include the need to position your car correctly, adjust your speed and stop if necessary

- significance of advance warning signs and road markings and acting correctly on what you see

- rules of priority, especially when dealing with unmarked junctions

- importance of good observation.

Remember, you need to look both ways, even if you're turning left – there may be another vehicle on your side of the road.

What if a pedestrian is crossing the road into which I am turning?

You should be checking as you approach the turning. A pedestrian who has already started to cross has priority, so give way. Remember, they might not have seen you.

How can I improve my view of the road into which I'm turning?

Sometimes buildings, hedges, bends in the road or parked cars can obscure your view. Edge forward slowly until you can see the road clearly before you pull out.

Tips from the experts

In a one-way street, move into the correct lane as soon as you can do so safely.

When approaching a junction make sure that you slow down in good time so that you don't have to brake harshly if you need to stop.

Watch out for pedestrians, cyclists and motorcyclists when you're turning as they're not as easy to see as larger vehicles.

What to expect on test

Your examiner will watch carefully to take account of your

- use of the MSM and PSL routines
- position and speed on approach to the junctions
- observation and judgement.

Usually when emerging from a junction, if you're turning left, keep well to the left but if you're turning right, keep as close to the centre of the road as is safe.

Recap questions

Q1 *When can you wait on the yellow criss-cross lines at a box junction?*

Q2 *Who has priority if there are no road markings at a crossroads?*

Q3 *How should you negotiate a traffic-light-controlled junction which has an advanced stop line for cyclists?*

Accompanying driver advice | **p97**

Keep a record

Notes

Your instructor should keep a record of your progress on your *Driver's Record*. You may also like to fill in your progress below and make any notes that might help you in this space:

| 1 ✓ introduced | 3 ✓ prompted | 5 independent |
| 2 ✓ full instruction | 4 ✓ seldom prompted | |

References | **HC** r170-183 | **DES** s8

Roundabouts

To deal with roundabouts safely and confidently you should have a thorough understanding of the rules which apply when approaching and negotiating them.

> You need to be able to do the following **consistently** and **without any help:**

LEVEL 5 Safely negotiate different types of roundabouts

To do this you need to be confident at dealing with these junctions...

- **standard roundabouts** – you should know how to approach and negotiate roundabouts even when there are no road markings directing you into particular lanes

- **mini-roundabouts** – you will probably need to adjust your speed on approach because there is less room to manoeuvre and less time to signal

- **multiple and satellite roundabouts** – assess the layout of the roundabouts by looking at the signs on approach. Treat each roundabout separately and apply the normal rules

- **traffic-light-controlled roundabouts** – priorities will often be different from normal roundabouts here.

LEVEL 5 Understand the rules for dealing with roundabouts

To do this you need to be aware of...

- how and when to apply the MSM and PSL routines (see page 30)

- the importance of effective observation and awareness of the traffic around you

- how to position your car correctly and which lane to use, both as you approach and when you are on a roundabout

- who has priority when you are entering a roundabout

- the procedure for leaving a roundabout.

Remember, look at all the road signs and markings and make sure you get into the correct lane for the direction you want to take in good time.

What if there is a long vehicle at the roundabout?

Stay well back and give them plenty of room, they might need to take a different course as they approach and go around the roundabout.

When should I start indicating to show I'm taking an exit?

You need to turn your left indicator on just after you have passed the exit before the one that you want to take. Remember to cancel it once you have finished turning.

Tips from the experts

Approach the roundabout at the correct speed so that you can assess other traffic using the roundabout. If you need to stop, avoid braking harshly.

Roundabouts are there to help traffic move freely. Don't stop unless you need to.

If you're in a queue, don't move forward before checking that the vehicle in front of you is moving. They may be more hesitant than you.

What to expect on test

Your examiner will take account of your ability to deal with roundabouts without undue hesitation. This will include your use of the MSM and PSL routines, your position, speed on approach, observation and judgement throughout.

Recap question

Q1 *Why would a cyclist signal right but stay in the left-hand lane as they approach a roundabout?*

Accompanying driver advice | p99

Keep a record

Notes

Your instructor should keep a record of your progress on your *Driver's Record*. You may also like to fill in your progress below and make any notes that might help you in this space:

1	introduced
2	full instruction
3	prompted
4	seldom prompted
5	independent

References

HC r184-190   **DES** s8

Dual carriageways

You join some dual carriageways from a slip road, in a similar way to joining a motorway. You should be confident using these high-speed roads where traffic can cross and turn right.

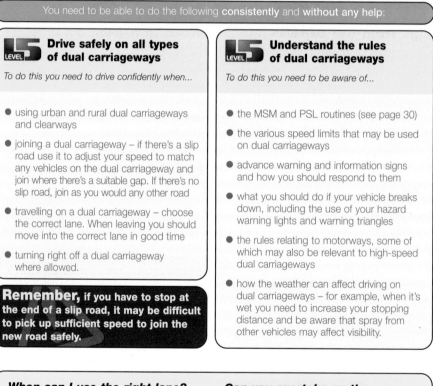

You need to be able to do the following **consistently** and **without any help**:

LEVEL 5 Drive safely on all types of dual carriageways

To do this you need to drive confidently when...

- using urban and rural dual carriageways and clearways

- joining a dual carriageway – if there's a slip road use it to adjust your speed to match any vehicles on the dual carriageway and join where there's a suitable gap. If there's no slip road, join as you would any other road

- travelling on a dual carriageway – choose the correct lane. When leaving you should move into the correct lane in good time

- turning right off a dual carriageway where allowed.

Remember, if you have to stop at the end of a slip road, it may be difficult to pick up sufficient speed to join the new road safely.

LEVEL 5 Understand the rules of dual carriageways

To do this you need to be aware of...

- the MSM and PSL routines (see page 30)

- the various speed limits that may be used on dual carriageways

- advance warning and information signs and how you should respond to them

- what you should do if your vehicle breaks down, including the use of your hazard warning lights and warning triangles

- the rules relating to motorways, some of which may also be relevant to high-speed dual carriageways

- how the weather can affect driving on dual carriageways – for example, when it's wet you need to increase your stopping distance and be aware that spray from other vehicles may affect visibility.

When can I use the right lane?

On some dual carriageways the lane on the right may be used for traffic turning right as well as for overtaking. If you're overtaking, watch for clues that traffic ahead of you is slowing down to turn right.

Can you overtake on the nearside of another vehicle?

You shouldn't normally overtake on the left, but you can if the traffic is moving slowly in queues and the queue in the right-hand lane is moving more slowly.

Tips from the experts

If there's no slip road, join as you would any other road. If you're turning right onto a dual carriageway, make sure that the central reservation is deep enough to protect your vehicle. If it isn't, you'll have to wait until the carriageway is clear in both directions before you start to cross.

When travelling on a high-speed dual carriageway, remember that situations can change very quickly – use your mirrors constantly so that you always know what is happening around you.

What to expect on test

Where possible your examiner will take you onto a high-speed road and watch to make sure that you join the road safely, use your mirrors effectively, and drive according to the higher speed of traffic around you.

If you have to use an emergency phone, stand so that you're facing the traffic on your side of the road. You need to be able to see traffic as it approaches.

Recap questions

Q1 *Which lane should you normally drive in when travelling on a dual carriageway?*

Q2 *If you break down on a dual carriageway, how far away from your vehicle should you place a warning triangle?*

Accompanying driver advice | p100

Keep a record

Your instructor should keep a record of your progress on your *Driver's Record*. You may also like to fill in your progress below and make any notes that might help you in this space:

1 introduced
2 full instruction
3 prompted
4 seldom prompted
5 independent

Notes

References **HC** r137-138, 173, 274   **DES** s8

Pedestrian crossings

You should be aware of the basic rules which apply to all pedestrian crossings but you also need to know the differences between each type of crossing.

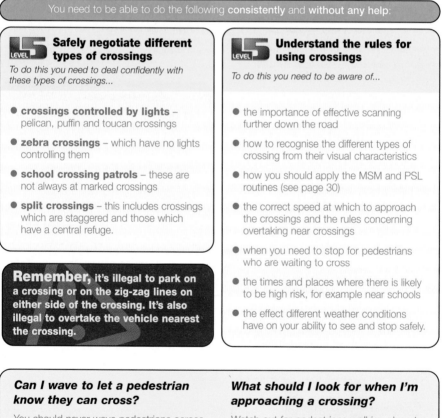

You need to be able to do the following **consistently** and **without any help**:

LEVEL 5 — Safely negotiate different types of crossings

To do this you need to deal confidently with these types of crossings...

- **crossings controlled by lights** – pelican, puffin and toucan crossings

- **zebra crossings** – which have no lights controlling them

- **school crossing patrols** – these are not always at marked crossings

- **split crossings** – this includes crossings which are staggered and those which have a central refuge.

Remember, it's illegal to park on a crossing or on the zig-zag lines on either side of the crossing. It's also illegal to overtake the vehicle nearest the crossing.

LEVEL 5 — Understand the rules for using crossings

To do this you need to be aware of...

- the importance of effective scanning further down the road

- how to recognise the different types of crossing from their visual characteristics

- how you should apply the MSM and PSL routines (see page 30)

- the correct speed at which to approach the crossings and the rules concerning overtaking near crossings

- when you need to stop for pedestrians who are waiting to cross

- the times and places where there is likely to be high risk, for example near schools

- the effect different weather conditions have on your ability to see and stop safely.

Can I wave to let a pedestrian know they can cross?

You should never wave pedestrians across in front of you as you could lead them into danger. Let them decide for themselves when it's safe to cross.

What should I look for when I'm approaching a crossing?

Watch out for pedestrians walking close to crossings, especially zebra crossings, as they may start to cross without looking at the traffic.

Tips from the experts

Make sure you approach all crossings at a speed which allows you to stop safely if you need to.

As you approach a zebra crossing, make sure you are aware of all pedestrians who may be intending to use the crossing.

Be patient when you're waiting at a crossing. Don't try to hurry those who are crossing by revving your engine, sounding your horn or edging forward.

What to expect on test

Your examiner will watch carefully to take account of how you deal with pedestrian crossings during your test. This includes how you prepare on the approach to crossings even when you do not have to stop to let pedestrians cross.

If you are waiting in a queue of traffic, don't straddle a crossing. Hold back as someone may want to cross before you are able to move off. At a controlled crossing the lights might change.

Recap questions

Q1 *Which type of crossing has a flashing amber phase, and what does it mean for you as a driver?*

Q2 *What do the zig-zag lines at a crossing mean?*

Accompanying driver advice | p101

Keep a record

Notes

Your instructor should keep a record of your progress on your *Driver's Record*. You may also like to fill in your progress below and make any notes that might help you in this space:

1 ✓ introduced	3 ✓ prompted	5
2 ✓ full instruction	4 ✓ seldom prompted	independent

References | **HC** r191-199 | **DES** s7

Turning the vehicle around

To turn your vehicle around it's often easiest and safest to use a roundabout or reverse into a side street. However, if these options aren't available, you may need to turn in the road.

You need to be able to do the following **consistently** and **without any help:**

LEVEL 5 **Safely turn your vehicle around in the road**

To do this you need to be confident performing this manoeuvre on...

- a narrow or wide road – try not to touch the kerbs at the end of each part of the manoeuvre

- a flat road or one with a camber – make sure you don't hit the kerb

- all appropriate types of road – choose a quiet road where you have a good view in all directions.

Remember, always start to turn your wheels in the opposite direction just before you stop. Don't steer while the car is stationary – this is called dry steering and can damage your tyres and steering.

LEVEL 5 **Understand what affects how you turn in the road**

To do this you need to be able to...

- observe carefully all around throughout the manoeuvre, especially checking your blind spots

- co-ordinate the hand and foot controls so that your vehicle moves smoothly

- steer in the correct manner while turning as tightly as possible

- use your judgement to perform this manoeuvre accurately

- avoid becoming a danger or obstruction to other road users – don't take too long to complete the turn

- choose a place to turn that is safe, legal and convenient where you have plenty of room and there's no obstruction in the road or on the pavement.

What if I can't turn around in three turns?

Depending on the width of the road, how difficult your vehicle is to steer and the length of your vehicle, you may need to make more turns.

Do I need to use the parking brake?

You may need to use the parking brake to prevent the car from rolling forward or backward if there is a pronounced camber or slope on the road.

Turn to the right and then briskly to the left just before you stop.

Turn to the left and then briskly to the right just before you stop.

Straighten up and make sure that you stay on your side of the road.

Tips from the experts

Check the road is clear in both directions before you start to move across.

The key is to keep the vehicle moving slowly while steering briskly.

What to expect on test

If you're asked to do this, your examiner will indicate a suitable place and ask you to pull up and turn your car around in the road.

Your examiner will be watching to see that you can turn your car around without hitting the kerbs, that you are aware of the situation around you, and are considerate to other road users.

Recap question

Q1 *What might you damage on your car if you turn the steering wheel while the car is stationary?*

Accompanying driver advice | p102

Keep a record

Notes

Your instructor should keep a record of your progress on your *Driver's Record*. You may also like to fill in your progress below and make any notes that might help you in this space:

1 ✓ introduced

2 ✓ full instruction

3 ✓ prompted

4 ✓ seldom prompted

5 independent

References **HC** r200 **DES** s9

Reversing

You should be able to reverse smoothly and safely while under complete control. This includes reversing to the left and right around sweeping curves and sharp corners.

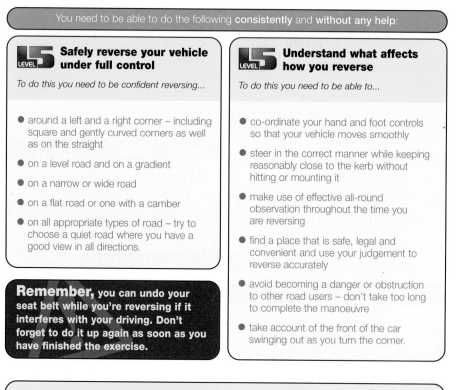

You need to be able to do the following **consistently** and **without any help**:

LEVEL 5 — Safely reverse your vehicle under full control

To do this you need to be confident reversing...

- around a left and a right corner – including square and gently curved corners as well as on the straight
- on a level road and on a gradient
- on a narrow or wide road
- on a flat road or one with a camber
- on all appropriate types of road – try to choose a quiet road where you have a good view in all directions.

Remember, you can undo your seat belt while you're reversing if it interferes with your driving. Don't forget to do it up again as soon as you have finished the exercise.

LEVEL 5 — Understand what affects how you reverse

To do this you need to be able to...

- co-ordinate your hand and foot controls so that your vehicle moves smoothly
- steer in the correct manner while keeping reasonably close to the kerb without hitting or mounting it
- make use of effective all-round observation throughout the time you are reversing
- find a place that is safe, legal and convenient and use your judgement to reverse accurately
- avoid becoming a danger or obstruction to other road users – don't take too long to complete the manoeuvre
- take account of the front of the car swinging out as you turn the corner.

Where should I look when I'm reversing?

Look mainly out of the back window, but don't forget to check all around throughout the time you're reversing and particularly at the point of turn.

How far should I aim to be from the kerb?

Keep parallel and reasonably close to the kerb all the time you're reversing.

Your car will swing out at the front as you reverse around the corner. Keep a good lookout for traffic and pedestrians in both roads.

Tips from the experts

As you reverse, keep a good lookout for traffic and pedestrians, especially in the road into which you are reversing.

Finish by straightening up your car and continue to reverse for a reasonable distance along the road into which you have reversed.

What to expect on test

Your examiner will ask you to pull up just before a side road on your left if they want you to reverse into it.

You may be asked to reverse into a road on your right if your view to the rear is restricted, as when you're in a van.

Your examiner will watch to make sure you reverse under full control keeping reasonably close to the kerb. They will assess your observation and responses to other road users.

Recap questions

Q1 *How would other road users know that you intend to reverse?*

Q2 *Into what type of road should you not reverse?*

Accompanying driver advice | **p103**

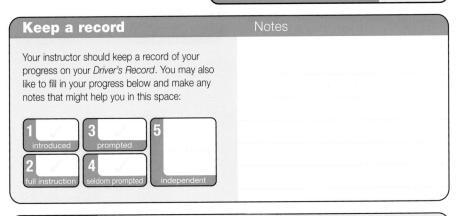

Keep a record

Your instructor should keep a record of your progress on your *Driver's Record*. You may also like to fill in your progress below and make any notes that might help you in this space:

| 1 introduced | 3 prompted | 5 |
| 2 full instruction | 4 seldom prompted | independent |

Notes

References | **HC** r200-203 | **DES** s9

Parking

Whether you're parking at the side of the road or using a bay in a car park, you need to gain the skills to do this safely before you drive on your own.

> You need to be able to do the following **consistently** and **without any help**:

L5 Safely reverse your vehicle into a parked position

To park at the side of the road or in a parking bay you need to be able to...

- co-ordinate your hand and foot controls well so that your car moves smoothly, whether on level ground or a slope

- steer in the correct manner, keeping a reasonable distance from other vehicles

- observe carefully all around while you are manoeuvring

- use your judgement to perform this manoeuvre accurately, signalling where it is necessary

- avoid becoming a danger or obstruction to other road users – don't take too long to complete the exercise.

L5 Understand how you should park your vehicle

To do this you need to be aware of...

- the need to check all around for other road users to make sure that you can reverse correctly and safely – don't just rely on your mirrors

- how to steer correctly – always try to steer when your car is moving. Avoid steering harshly while the car is stationary.

Remember, you need to choose a place to park that is safe, legal and convenient. You can check these in The Official Highway Code.

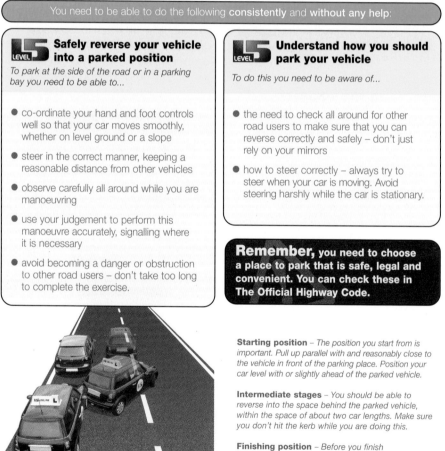

Starting position – *The position you start from is important. Pull up parallel with and reasonably close to the vehicle in front of the parking place. Position your car level with or slightly ahead of the parked vehicle.*

Intermediate stages – *You should be able to reverse into the space behind the parked vehicle, within the space of about two car lengths. Make sure you don't hit the kerb while you are doing this.*

Finishing position – *Before you finish manoeuvring make sure your car is reasonably close to and parallel with the kerb.*

Look at the layout of the markings and the space available and decide the easiest way to park.

Constantly look all round to check that you're not in danger of hitting pedestrians or other cars.

Make sure you straighten your wheels before you finish and that you end up squarely parked.

Tips from the experts

When parking in a bay there may be times when the layout would make it easier to turn first so that you can back into the parking space.

What to expect on test

You may not have to do this exercise on test, but if you do your examiner will ask you to pull up at the side of the road.

They will explain that you will need to park behind a parked car. Alternatively you could be asked to park in a bay at the beginning or end of your test.

Recap questions

Q1 *Give examples of road markings which indicate you mustn't park at any time.*

Q2 *What's the minimum distance you should park away from a junction?*

Accompanying driver advice   p104

Keep a record

Notes

Your instructor should keep a record of your progress on your *Driver's Record*. You may also like to fill in your progress below and make any notes that might help you in this space:

| 1 ✓ introduced | 3 ✓ prompted | 5 independent |
| 2 ✓ full instruction | 4 ✓ seldom prompted | |

References   **HC** r202, 238-252   **DES** s9

Emergency stop

Effective scanning and reading of the road ahead will cut down the risk of having to make an emergency stop. If it's unavoidable, brake as quickly as possible while keeping the car under full control.

LEVEL 5 Safely stop your car as quickly as possible

To be able to do this while keeping full control you need to know...

- how to co-ordinate the brake and clutch pedals so that the car comes to a halt under full control

- the effect of ABS brakes – you need to know how to tell whether the car you're driving has ABS brakes as this will affect the way you use the brake and clutch

- how different road and weather conditions can affect the way you stop safely

- how to control a skid if one occurs

- how to move away safely again after you've made an emergency stop.

Remember, although you need to know how to stop safely in an emergency, it's important that you know how to avoid having to do so by using your hazard perception skills to plan ahead. You should always drive in such a way that you're aware of situations that might develop and have time to respond to them safely.

 ABS

Look for this symbol on your dashboard, it should light up when you turn on the ignition.

What should I do if my car starts to skid?

If you don't have ABS brakes, first release the pressure on the brake pedal. If the rear of the car starts to slide sideways, steer gently in the same direction as the skid.

How do I know whether the car I'm driving has ABS?

There will be a warning light on the dashboard and advice will be given in the handbook. Also, ask your instructor to demonstrate how ABS works.

Tips from the experts

React quickly, keep both hands on the wheel and try to stop in a straight line without allowing the car to swing off course.

Know the car you're driving – if the car has ABS brakes, make sure that you've read the handbook and know what to do, as advice can differ between manufacturers.

If you have to do this on test, don't try to anticipate the signal which the examiner will give you.

What to expect on test

You may not have to do this exercise on test, but if you do your examiner will ask you to pull up at the side of the road. Your examiner will then explain the exercise and show you what the signal will be.

When your examiner gives the signal, try to stop the car as you would in a real emergency. They will check the road behind to make sure it's safe before giving the signal to stop.

Recap questions

Q1 *What happens if the wheels lock?*

Q2 *In what conditions would ABS brakes not work as effectively as they would normally?*

Accompanying driver advice | p105

Keep a record

Notes

Your instructor should keep a record of your progress on your *Driver's Record*. You may also like to fill in your progress below and make any notes that might help you in this space:

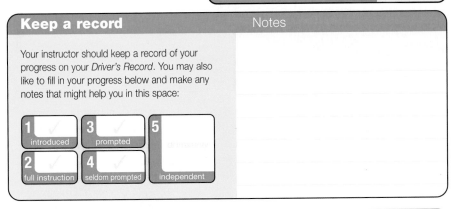

1 introduced	3 prompted	5
2 full instruction	4 seldom prompted	independent

References | HC r117-120 | DES s5

Independent driving

Driving independently gives you the chance to experience what it will be like to drive after you have passed your test. You can acquire this key skill while learning so that you are ready to drive alone.

You need to be able to do the following **consistently** and **without any help**:

L5 Drive independently

LEVEL

To do this confidently while keeping full control you need to

- plan ahead so that you don't have to make any late actions
- be able to follow direction signs
- use the MSM and PSL routines (page 30)
- position your car correctly in good time
- understand the correct use of lanes both with and without directional information
- respond correctly to other road users
- know and respond to traffic signs and road markings.

Remember, you will not be prompted when to begin the MSM-PSL routine. Plan well ahead and start the routine in good time.

What will happen if I go off route?

If you take a wrong turning, keep calm. Your examiner will guide you back onto the original route and make sure you know where you are expected to go.

How will I know where to turn?

Your examiner will ask you to pull up and then will either ask you to follow the road signs for a destination, such as the town centre, or you will be shown a simple map indicating the route you should follow.

Tips from the experts

Look and plan well ahead. Give signals in good time but not too early or you may mislead other road users, especially if there is another turning before your junction.

If you realise you are taking the wrong turning don't make a sudden change of direction as this could cause a collision. It is better to complete the turn safely and then find somewhere safe to turn around and rejoin your route.

What to expect on test

Your examiner will give you directions either using a simplified map as shown opposite, or ask you to follow road signs. You will be asked to repeat the directions to make sure you have understood them. Your examiner will be watching how you

- apply the MSM and PSL routines
- plan your driving
- respond to traffic signs and road markings
- interact with other road users
- control your car.

Recap questions

Q1 *How do I know when to start driving independently?*

Q2 *Will I be told which lane to use?*

Accompanying driver advice   p106

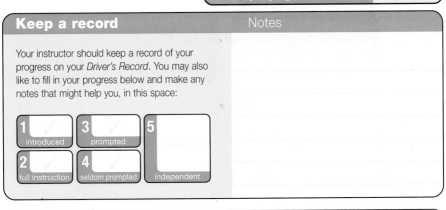

Keep a record

Your instructor should keep a record of your progress on your *Driver's Record*. You may also like to fill in your progress below and make any notes that might help you, in this space:

1 introduced
2 full instruction
3 prompted
4 seldom prompted
5 independent

Notes

References   **HC** r170-190   **DES** s7

Darkness

There are many factors that make driving in the dark more hazardous. Judging speed at night can be difficult, so be particularly careful at junctions.

> You need to be able to do the following **consistently** and **without any help**:

L5 Drive safely in darkness on all types of roads

To do this you need to be confident on...

- **urban roads** – the variety of different lights such as vehicle lights, street lights, shop signs - can be distracting

- **rural roads** – the main source of light will be your headlights

- **single and dual carriageways** – there may be a mixture of lighting on these roads.

L5 Understand the effects of darkness

To do this you need to be aware of...

- how darkness affects your visibility and therefore your speed and stopping distance, especially in bad weather

- when you need to use your lights, which lights to use and the importance of keeping them clean

- the rules concerning the use of your horn at night

- how to park safely and legally when it is dark.

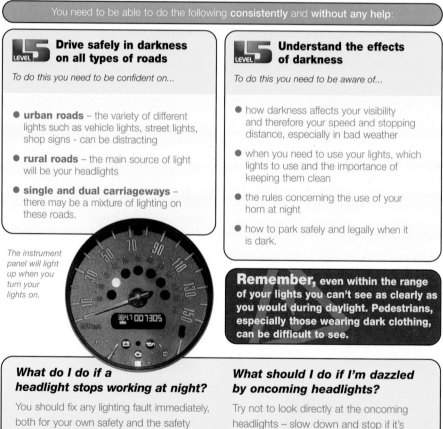

The instrument panel will light up when you turn your lights on.

Remember, even within the range of your lights you can't see as clearly as you would during daylight. Pedestrians, especially those wearing dark clothing, can be difficult to see.

What do I do if a headlight stops working at night?

You should fix any lighting fault immediately, both for your own safety and the safety of others. Don't forget to carry a spare set of bulbs with you, if appropriate for the vehicle.

What should I do if I'm dazzled by oncoming headlights?

Try not to look directly at the oncoming headlights – slow down and stop if it's necessary. Don't retaliate by leaving your headlights on full beam to dazzle the oncoming driver.

You should always use headlights in the dark, even when you're driving in built up areas.

Tips from the experts

You should always drive so that you can stop safely within the distance you can see to be clear. At night this means within the range of your lights.

Your lights are there to help you to be seen by others as well as to help you see. Make sure you switch your headlights on in good time as it starts to get dark and that you don't switch them off as it gets lighter until you're sure it's safe.

When following or meeting other vehicles, dip your headlights so that they don't dazzle other drivers.

Judging speed and distance at night can be difficult. Be particularly careful at junctions.

What to expect on test

If conditions require it your examiner will watch to make sure that you

- use your lights correctly
- drive within the distance you can see to be clear.

Recap questions

Q1 *At night, when can you park on the side of the road without any lights?*

Q2 *When must you not use your horn at night?*

Accompanying driver advice   **p107**

Keep a record

Your instructor should keep a record of your progress on your *Driver's Record*. You may also like to fill in your progress below and make any notes that might help you, in this space:

1 introduced

2 full instruction

3 prompted

4 seldom prompted

5 independent

Notes

References   **HC** r112-115, 248-252   **DES** s13

Weather conditions

You need to be aware of the effect some weather conditions such as fog and low sun can have on visibility. Other conditions, such as ice, snow and rain, can affect the way that your vehicle handles.

You need to be able to do the following **consistently** and **without any help**:

LEVEL 5 — Drive safely in all weather conditions

To do this you need to be confident in these weather conditions...

- **fog** – remember, fog is often patchy so your level of visibility can change very quickly

- **ice and snow** – check weather forecasts and only travel if it's absolutely necessary

- **bright sunshine** – be aware of the glare this may cause, especially when the road is wet or the sun is low

- **wind** – you may be affected by gusts of wind around buildings, bridges, etc

- **rain** – wet roads mean longer stopping distances. Your visibility may be affected by spray from other vehicles.

LEVEL 5 — Understand how to deal with weather conditions

To do this on all types of road in urban and rural areas you need to be aware of...

- how different weather conditions will affect your visibility, speed and stopping distance. You need to demonstrate that you can respond to these conditions safely

- how the condition and characteristics of your vehicle can affect its handling

- the warning signs and signals that may be used

- how to avoid skidding and aquaplaning, and how to control them if they do occur

- when to use your lights and which lights to use in poor visibility.

Remember, when the roads are wet, your stopping distance may be doubled. In icy conditions you may need to allow 10 times the normal stopping distance.

Be aware that after heavy rain the water in a ford is likely to be much higher.

Ford

What if it becomes foggy?

Slow right down, it's much more difficult to judge distances and the speed of other vehicles in fog. Use dipped headlights or fog lights when visibility is seriously reduced.

What do I do if the road is flooded?

Stop and assess how deep the water is. If the water's not too deep, drive on slowly. Remember to test your brakes afterwards.

Tips from the experts

Always keep your windscreen, mirrors and windows clean and clear so that you can see as much as possible all around.

You may not be affected by high winds, but be aware that other road users such as cyclists, motorcyclists and drivers of high-sided vehicles are more vulnerable and may be blown into your path.

When visibility is reduced by fog, use dipped headlights and, if the distance you can see falls below 100 metres (328 feet), use your front and rear fog lights. If you do use fog lights, remember to switch them off when visibility improves.

It's not only bad weather that can cause difficult driving conditions. The glare of the sun – especially when the sun is low in the sky in winter – can make it very difficult to see other road users.

What to expect on test

Your examiner will watch to make sure that you drive according to the weather conditions prevailing during the test.

Recap questions

Q1 *How can you tell that you're aquaplaning, and what should you do to regain control?*

Q2 *Why is it dangerous to leave your rear fog lights on if conditions improve?*

Accompanying driver advice   p108

Keep a record

Notes

Your instructor should keep a record of your progress on your *Driver's Record*. You may also like to fill in your progress below and make any notes that might help you, in this space:

1	✓	introduced
2	✓	full instruction
3	✓	prompted
4	✓	seldom prompted
5		independent

| **References** | **HC** r226-237 | **DES** s12 |

Environmental issues

Everything from the type of car and its fuel consumption to the way in which you drive influences the environment. You need to understand how to minimise the negative effects.

You need to be able to do the following **consistently** and **without any help**:

LEVEL 5 Understand how driving affects the environment

To do this you need to be aware of...

- **air pollution** – the effect that vehicle exhaust gases have on the climate, your health and the health and safety of others. Understand the beneficial effect of catalytic converters on the environment

- **noise pollution** – try to avoid making unnecessary noise, especially when travelling at night or in residential areas.

LEVEL 5 Minimise your effect on the environment

To do this you need to know how you can...

- change your driving style so that you cause less damage to the environment

- maintain your vehicle in a good condition to make it run more efficiently

- dispose of vehicle waste such as spent oil, old batteries and used tyres correctly

- reduce your fuel consumption by limiting your use of air conditioning and removing any unnecessary load

- use the highest possible gear without making the engine struggle.

It's illegal to pour oil down the drain – *you need to dispose of it correctly.*

WASTE OIL

Remember, many of the suggestions for reducing environmental impact will also reduce your motoring costs.

Does my speed really affect my fuel consumption?

Yes, it makes a big difference. If you travel at 70 mph (112 km/h) you're likely to use up to 30% more fuel than if you covered the same distance at 50 mph (80 km/h).

Does the car I buy make a big difference?

Try to choose a vehicle with low fuel consumption. For further information about fuel and CO_2 emissions, check the website **vcacarfueldata.org.uk**

Tips from the experts

Use your hazard perception skills to plan ahead so that you can avoid harsh braking and acceleration. Driving smoothly can reduce your fuel consumption by about 15% as well as reducing the wear and tear on your vehicle.

Reverse into a parking space so that you can drive out of it. Manoeuvring when the engine is cold uses lots of fuel. Don't over-rev your engine in low gear.

Check tyre pressures regularly. Incorrect tyre pressure results in a shorter tyre life and may be dangerous. Under-inflated tyres can increase fuel consumption.

Try to avoid using your car for very short journeys, especially when the engine is cold. Also, consider car-sharing or using public transport where you can.

Avoid carrying unnecessary weight and remove a roof rack when it's not being used. The drag on a roof box can add up to 15% on fuel consumption.

What to expect on test

You will be asked questions which test your understanding of environmental issues during your theory test.

Recap question

Q1 *Why are catalytic converters fitted?*

Accompanying driver advice p109

Keep a record

Notes

Your instructor should keep a record of your progress on your *Driver's Record*. You may also like to fill in your progress below and make any notes that might help you, in this space:

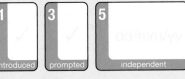

1	3	5
✓	✓	dd/mm/yy
introduced	prompted	independent

References **HC** r123 **DES** s17

Passengers and loads

As a driver you need to understand the responsibilities that you have to any passengers, whether they are adults or children, and also how to secure any items that you are transporting.

You need to be able to do the following **consistently** and **without any help**:

LEVEL 5 — Carrying passengers and loads safely

To do this you need to know...

- your responsibility as a driver regarding carrying passengers (other adults, children and babies) and animals in your car safely
- the safest way to carry loads in and on your car
- how to load trailers safely and carry bicycles on your car.

LEVEL 5 — Understand the rules of carrying passengers and loads

To do this you must be aware of...

- the rules concerning the use of seat belts, especially when you are responsible
- the importance of not putting a rear-facing baby seat into a seat which is protected by an airbag
- the importance of checking that all doors are shut properly and that animals are safely restrained in a purpose-made carry box or behind a guard
- how to stow luggage or load it securely and the importance of distributing weight evenly.

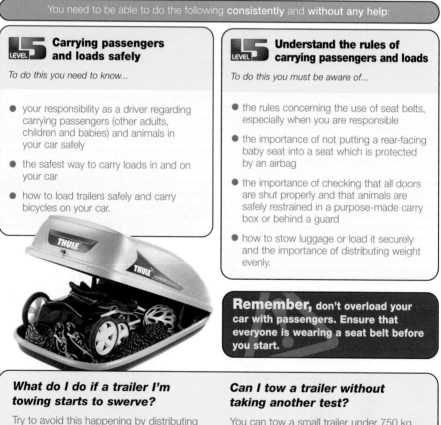

Remember, don't overload your car with passengers. Ensure that everyone is wearing a seat belt before you start.

What do I do if a trailer I'm towing starts to swerve?

Try to avoid this happening by distributing the weight properly in the trailer. If it does happen, ease off the accelerator to reduce speed gently.

Can I tow a trailer without taking another test?

You can tow a small trailer under 750 kg maximum authorised mass without having to take another test. You may also be able to tow a larger trailer (see pages 129–137).

Tips from the experts

Specially designed roof boxes are streamlined so they will save fuel as well as securing the load safely.

Special cycle racks fitted on top of or behind the car allow you to carry cycles securely – if they are fitted behind the car, make sure that the number plates and lights can still be seen clearly.

If you are carrying a load, make sure it is secure and that it doesn't stick out dangerously.

Any load will have an effect on the handling of your car – changes to the weight and centre of gravity will affect the steering and braking. Allow more stopping distance when you are carrying a heavy load – you may also need to inflate your tyres more and adjust your headlights (see your car's handbook).

What to expect on test

You will be asked questions about passengers and carrying loads during your theory test.

Recap questions

Q1 *Who is responsible for ensuring that children under 14 wear a seat belt?*

Q2 *What's the speed limit for a car towing a trailer travelling on a single carriageway road?*

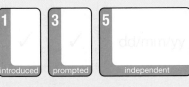

As the driver
you're responsible for ensuring that any baby or young child is wearing an appropriate restraint.

Accompanying driver advice p110

Keep a record

Your instructor should keep a record of your progress on your *Driver's Record*. You may also like to fill in your progress below and make any notes that might help you, in this space:

1	3	5
✓	✓	dd/mm/yy
introduced	prompted	independent

Notes

References **HC** r99-102   **DES** s2

Security

This covers not only the security of your vehicle but also its contents and your personal security. You need to be aware of the ways in which you can reduce the risks.

You need to be able to do the following **consistently** and **without any help**:

L5 Understand the importance of personal safety

To do this you need to be aware of...

- the need to stay alert at all times
- the importance of letting someone know where you're going and when you expect to arrive or return
- why you should not leave important or valuable items on display in your car
- the need to choose a sensible place to leave your car, especially at night.

L5 Understand the importance of vehicle security

To do this you must be aware of...

- how to find a safe place to park
- the different types of security measures available such as steering wheel locks and immobilisers.

Remember, if possible, park your car in an attended or Secure Car Park. For information and to search for secured sites visit securedcarparks.com

This is one of the measures you can use to improve the security of your vehicle.

When should I lock away my valuables?

Criminals could be observing your actions in the car park. Try to lock valuables away before leaving home.

Where can I get advice about vehicle security?

Speak to your local crime prevention officer who will advise you on devices and any vehicle watch schemes that may operate in your area.

Tips from the experts

An alarm or immobiliser, a visible security device such as a steering wheel lock or having the registration number etched on all the windows can deter a would-be thief.

Before you leave your car, make sure that you remove all valuables (or at least lock them out of sight), close all the windows and then lock the door.

If you have to park on the side of the road at night, leave your car in a well-lit area.

Carry a mobile phone so that you can use it to call for help if you break down, are involved in an incident or feel threatened in any way.

Always lock your car even if it is for a short time, such as when paying for petrol.

What to expect on test

You will be asked questions about vehicle security during your theory test.

Recap question

Q1 *What measures can you take to protect your personal safety when parking at night?*

Accompanying driver advice | p111

Keep a record

Notes

Your instructor should keep a record of your progress on your *Driver's Record*. You may also like to fill in your progress below and make any notes that might help you, in this space:

1	3	5
✓	✓	dd/mm/yy
introduced	prompted	independent

References | **HC** r239, p131 | **DES** s20

section **three**
ACCOMPANYING DRIVER ADVICE

This section covers
- Accompanying a learner
- Getting started
- Attitude
- Planning
- Legal responsibilities
- Cockpit checks

- Safety checks
- Controls and instruments
- Moving away and stopping
- Safe positioning
- Mirrors – vision and use
- Signals
- Anticipation and planning
- Use of speed
- Other traffic
- Junctions
- Roundabouts
- Dual carriageways
- Pedestrian crossings
- Turning the vehicle around
- Reversing
- Parking
- Emergency stop
- Independent driving
- Darkness
- Weather conditions
- Environmental issues
- Passengers and loads
- Security

Accompanying a learner

When accompanying a learner, look on the process of making your relative or friend a safe driver as a team effort involving you, your learner and their ADI.

If you feel unsure about anything or want a bit of advice, you can talk to the ADI about the areas which concern you. You may want to accompany your learner on their next lesson to see how the ADI copes with situations you find difficult. Make sure your learner is happy for you to sit in and arrange a suitable time with the ADI.

Sometimes you may think the ADI is teaching a driving technique which seems wrong to you. Remember, as cars become more sophisticated, so recommended techniques change to take advantage of new technology.

The ADI is probably using the most up-to-date methods which may be different from the way you were taught. Don't confuse your learner by expecting them to do things 'your way'. One part of your role is to enable your learner to practise the techniques taught by their ADI.

> **Remember,** working together is the best way of ensuring everyone's aim of safe driving for life.

Getting started

Beginning

For a new driver there's an awful lot to learn. The list includes

- a good knowledge of driving theory
- learning how to operate a complicated set of controls (which looks so easy)
- operating the controls while putting the theory into practice
- developing good judgement
- anticipation and awareness.

As well as developing these skills the new driver needs to learn to cope with

- other road users
- the weather
- road conditions
- navigation.

> **Remember,** new drivers cannot begin driving until they have received their licence from the Driver and Vehicle Licensing Agency (DVLA) and it has come into effect.

Even after basic control skills have developed, being able to cope with constantly changing demands and unexpected events – often in a fraction of a second – is a skill that comes with experience.

The whole business is complicated, challenging and, for some, extremely difficult. To expect that all this can be learned in a few short lessons is a mistake.

A learner driver needs to gain enough skill and experience to enable them to drive alone safely once they have passed their driving test. As more miles are driven and more experience is gained, the novice driver will gradually progress towards becoming an experienced driver.

However, driving is a subject where there are always new lessons to be learned and it is a foolish and dangerous driver who thinks they know it all.

So how does a learner begin the process of going from novice to competent safe driver? The answer lies in two key areas

Training – to learn new skills

Practice – to gain experience.

Training

Most people learn to drive with an ADI. Driving instructors are professionals who are trained to teach driving skills in a structured manner to suit differing abilities.

Remember, some insurance companies don't insure people under 25 years of age, while others may offer reduced premiums for new drivers who complete the Pass Plus scheme (see page 122).

Don't risk driving uninsured!

Many pupils only have one or two hours of professional driving instruction each week and their experience is often limited to driving at the same time of day and over the same types of road.

Four levels of learning to drive

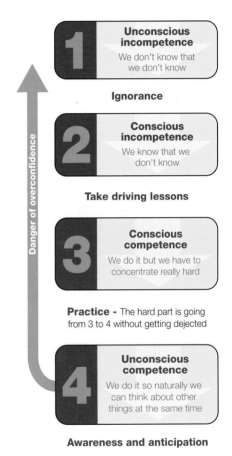

1 Unconscious incompetence
We don't know that we don't know

Ignorance

2 Conscious incompetence
We know that we don't know

Take driving lessons

3 Conscious competence
We do it but we have to concentrate really hard

Practice - The hard part is going from 3 to 4 without getting dejected

4 Unconscious competence
We do it so naturally we can think about other things at the same time

Awareness and anticipation

Danger of overconfidence

75

Where you fit in

As an accompanying driver you will be helping your learner have more practice and gain wider experience of the varied driving conditions they are likely to meet once they have passed their driving test.

However, there are a few things to consider before you start (see below).

Once you are ready to take on this responsibility you need to think about developing the skills of your learner – know their limits and don't attempt any driving which will be beyond their ability.

You're helping a new driver to gain skills which will help to keep them safe for many years to come.

That's not to say it will be an easy task and there may be times when you need to remind yourself why you're there.

> **Remember,** learners who combine extra practice with professional lessons not only perform better on their driving test but go on to have a reduced incident rate in the early years of driving unaccompanied.

Don't forget that only an ADI can charge for driving lessons. Even accepting money for fuel is an offence unless you're an ADI. Don't be caught out.

Can you do it legally?

Before you agree to accompany a learner driver there are a few things you need to check

1 Have you held a full EC/EEA driving licence for at least three years for the category of vehicle being driven?

2 Are you at least 21 years of age?

3 Is the car you intend to use insured for use by the learner?

4 Is the car fitted with L-plates (D-plates in Wales) to both the front and rear of the car?

5 Is the car you intend to use in a safe, roadworthy condition?

The answer must be YES to all questions before you can act as an accompanying driver to a learner.

What can you expect?

To start with, don't expect this to be easy. Learning to drive takes a lot longer than most people realise. You need to set aside plenty of time for practice sessions so there are no excuses.

If you set dates and times when you're expecting to go out with your learner, you're more likely to be in a calm frame of mind than if you've had to stop what you were doing and grudgingly give your time.

Be guided by the ADI, but once the basic skills have been learned, it's a good idea to let your learner do a lot of the everyday driving, such as to the shops or to school or college.

If your learner struggles with something you think is easy, don't worry. Everyone learns at different rates and in different ways and it may be necessary to go over the same ground many times.

Memory often plays tricks and you may have forgotten how you struggled with some aspects of learning to drive.

> **Remember,** young drivers are about twice as likely to be involved in a road traffic incident negotiating a bend than older drivers.

What are you expecting to achieve?

The goals you should be helping a new driver to achieve are

- confidence and competence in practising these new skills

- a sound basis on which to build their driving career

- enough experience to be able to think for themselves and cope safely with any driving situation they meet

- confidence about their ability to pass the driving test

- an understanding of their responsibility as a driver.

Some learners struggle with the clutch, while others have difficulty with the gears. The key is to be patient.

The practice vehicle

Is your car suitable for your learner to drive? – A learner may learn in any make or model of car but a large, powerful car may be more difficult to control than a smaller model.

Small cars are not necessarily any easier to drive but their size can make judging the car's position easier, especially during manoeuvres.

It might be helpful to find a driving school that uses a similar car to your own. If this isn't possible, make allowances for your learner if they struggle to adapt to your car after lessons in the school car.

Make sure the L (or D) plates are secure, as you don't want them to fly off once you try roads with higher speed limits.

Remember, fit an extra rear view mirror. Knowing what's going on behind is important for safety and peace of mind.

L plates – Avoid fixing L (D) plates to the windscreen or rear window since they restrict the view. Don't forget to cover or remove the L (D) plates when the car is being used by a full licence holder.

Attitude

Bad habits

It's too easy for bad habits to creep unnoticed into anyone's driving. Before you act as an accompanying driver, it's worth looking at your own driving. You'll have little credibility if you expect your learner to drive one way while you practise another – and don't expect your learner not to notice. Why not have a lesson or two with the ADI yourself? This will allow an expert to check your driving and help you to improve your skills.

Drinking and driving, speed limits, use of signals, seat belts and attitude to other road users are all aspects of driving where standards slip. Setting a good example when you drive will have positive benefits for both you and your learner.

Patience

Frustration can soon set in when your learner struggles with something you think should be easy, or can't do something that they could do the last time you went out. If something is proving difficult, don't keep trying it until tempers fray. Leave it and come back to it another time. Learning to drive should be an enjoyable experience, not an ordeal.

Other road users may be inconsiderate and show little regard for the fact that your driver is a learner. Don't allow this to wind you up since it will also affect your learner. Knocking a learner driver's confidence can ruin their driving career before it has even started.

Technique

Before accompanying your learner you should give some thought to how you are going to

- give directions
- cope with dangerous situations.

Remember, learning to drive takes a lot longer than most people think. **Be patient with your learner.**

Your learner will need clear directions given calmly and in plenty of time. You will need to look and think that bit further ahead than normal. If your learner has difficulty telling their right from their left you'll need to overcome this problem. Your ADI should be able to give you some advice on these matters, as well as tips on giving directions at any complex junctions in your area.

Safety is your priority and, where possible, you should act early and prevent hazards from developing into dangerous situations. If a dangerous situation does develop, you may need to

- speak firmly and clearly without shouting
- reach across and take control of the steering
- use the handbrake
- use dual controls if fitted.

Avoiding conflicts

Accompanying a novice driver can be frustrating, unnerving and a lot harder than you think. Here are a few points worth remembering to help you keep on top of it.

- Talking to the ADI will help you plan practice sessions which avoid areas that are too difficult for your learner's present level of ability.

- Learn from mistakes and don't dwell on them. Encouragement and tolerance will help skills and confidence develop.

- Nothing is achieved if you allow yourself to become angry with your learner. If it's all going wrong have a break for five minutes or stop the session altogether if things are too bad.

- If something happens which scares either of you, pull over and give yourselves time to calm down. Discuss what went wrong and why. Were you expecting too much from your learner?

- If another road user fails to show your learner due consideration, don't allow it to upset you. Set a good example, keep calm and turn the experience into a lesson in anticipation.

Remember, keep reminding yourself that you're making a big difference to your learner's long-term driving safety. Learners rarely have crashes while practising.

- Prevent your learner from getting into difficulties by looking well ahead so you can anticipate problems. Don't expect them to have the same degree of awareness and judgement as you.

- Your learner is going to drive in the way their instructor has taught. If any techniques differ from the way you drive, don't argue over who's right or insist they do it your way. Make a note and discuss it with the ADI.

Planning

When to start

DSA recommends that new drivers reach a level of proficiency with an ADI before starting to practise with an accompanying driver. Ask the ADI to tell you when your learner is ready to start practising. Starting too soon may be unnerving for both of you and could lead to anything from a loss of confidence through to a serious loss of control.

Remember, a learner driver may find driving very tiring. Many crashes involving young drivers result from lack of experience.

Use the *Driver's Record* to see the progress being made and the topics needing practice. To start with, this will be mostly control skills but will gradually move on to include the whole syllabus.

Early days

Before you begin your first practice sessions, you need to give some thought to where and when you're going to conduct them. When you begin, driving in heavy traffic at rush hour isn't going to be good for either of you.

Where – Pick a quiet area where

- there won't be much traffic to deal with
- you won't cause a nuisance to other road users or local residents.

It's also a good idea to find somewhere fairly level because of the added difficulties a hill can create at this stage.

Your learner will probably drive quite slowly and, despite your efforts to find somewhere quiet, you may find a queue of traffic building up behind. If this happens, be prepared to ask your learner to pull over somewhere safe and let it pass.

When – Plan the first few practice sessions to avoid busy times of the day. These include rush hours, school start and finish times or during local events.

Your learner can only practise when you make the time available. Work and other commitments may make demands on you and the only time you have could be evenings and weekends.

In the winter months, evening practice will be in the dark – but don't let this be an excuse not to practise. As long as the weather conditions aren't dangerous, practising in the dark shouldn't be a problem.

During – Remember that you are in charge of the vehicle even when the learner is driving. You need all your concentration for supervising the learner – you **MUST NOT** use your mobile phone or other hand-held device at any time while the provisional licence holder is driving a motor vehicle on a road (see page 19).

Planning your sessions

Many learners take their driving lessons at the same time of day and drive repeatedly over the same types of road.

> **Remember,** could your learner cope with any situation that might arise? They will have to when they pass their test.

While this may provide a level of familiarity with these roads, it does little to provide a broad experience of the wide variety of driving conditions your learner will meet when they have passed their test.

Good practice sessions should build both experience and confidence. This can be achieved by planning each session around your learner's requirements and their driving limitations. Refer to their *Driver's Record* to see which topics need practising.

As part of your planning you will need to think about routes, time of day, road types, manoeuvring and weather conditions. These are now looked at in turn.

Routes – Thinking through where you are going to take your learner will enable you to

- avoid areas which may have features such as a steep hill or a difficult junction which they are not yet ready to encounter
- practise certain aspects such as left turns, traffic lights, one way streets, etc.

You don't want to put your learner into a situation that they can't cope with and could have been avoided if you had planned ahead.

Time of day – Local knowledge will allow you to know which roads are busiest and when. This will allow you to avoid the worst areas in the early days, and practise in heavy traffic when your learner is ready.

Daylight, dusk and darkness are all driving conditions which need different skills and need to be practised. If your learner has great difficulty seeing at night, get their night vision tested by an optician. Your learner should be able to think independently and use the car's lights when necessary.

Road types – While a learner cannot use a motorway, they can drive on all other types of road. For example, driving on a dual carriageway calls for skills and techniques that will need to be learned and practised.

If a *Driver's Record* is being used it will indicate the types of road where practice is needed.

Manoeuvring – The driving test requires manoeuvres to be demonstrated which reflect real driving situations. These include stopping in an emergency, turning the car around in the road, reversing into a side road and parking using reverse gear, both on the road and into car park bays.

The ADI will teach the techniques and, if a *Driver's Record* is being used, will record which have been taught and which need practice.

Weather conditions – Many learners begin learning in the spring months and pass the driving test before winter arrives.

These learners may have had little or no experience of driving in

- rain and slippery conditions
- mist and fog
- windy conditions.

These are everyday conditions that most motorists encounter in their first year of driving. When the ADI indicates your learner is ready to cope with them, be prepared to go out in these conditions as they occur.

> **Remember,** don't underestimate the weather. Extreme weather can make driving unsafe and it's recommended that you avoid practising in these conditions in the early days.
>
> **If in doubt – don't venture out.**

Key skills

The following pages (84-111) give advice and tips about helping your learner practise the 24 key skills explained in Section two.

Legal responsibilities

Refer to p22

At **Level 5**, your learner should have a full understanding of their legal responsibilities as a driver. These include

- driving licences and accompanying learner drivers
- road tax (SORN), insurance and MOT
- health and eyesight
- New Drivers Act
- tiredness and rest periods
- traffic rules and regulations
- alcohol and drugs
- mobile phones
- vehicle condition
- dealing with road traffic incidents.

> **Remember,** ignorance is no excuse in the eyes of the law. Make sure you are both up to date.

How you can help

Ask questions so that your learner has to think about their responsibilities. If you are both unclear about an issue then work together to find out the facts. For example, if you didn't know about the New Drivers Act, you could ask your ADI to explain it to both of you.

To keep up to date with changes in the law, own and refer to the latest edition of *The Official Highway Code.*

What to expect

Many new drivers will have an understanding of the issues that directly affect them such as applying for a driving licence. They may not know about recent changes in the law or matters that you routinely deal with such as taxing your car.

If you involve your learner they may not only learn the processes but they may also appreciate the costs associated with owning and running a car.

Cockpit checks

Refer to | p24

Your learner will have reached **Level 5** for this topic when they independently

- make a point of checking their door is closed properly

- check and, if necessary, adjust their driving position. This includes adjusting the seat, steering wheel, head restraint, etc

- correctly fasten their seat belt

- check and adjust the mirrors

- check the handbrake is on and the gear lever is in neutral.

How you can help

Watch to see that your learner completes their checks before starting the engine. Look to see that each item is checked and not just mentioned.

What to expect

It is not uncommon for learners to find that once they are on the road, one or more mirrors require some further adjustment, or the seat needs re-positioning.

Do not let them try to make adjustments while on the move, but find a safe place for them to pull over and stop before making any further adjustment.

> **Remember,** mirrors need to be adjusted so that they can be used with the least possible head movement.

Safety checks

Refer to   p26

As part of their driving test your learner will be asked to show and explain basic safety checks necessary to keep their car safe on the road.

These questions are published on **direct.gov.uk/motoring**

The ADI will cover the driving test requirements but learning how to carry out routine safety checks is not something to learn for the test and then forget. Aspects such as tyre condition are the driver's responsibility and, if the tyres are illegal, the driver could be fined or have penalty points added to their driving licence.

How you can help

Before each practice drive watch while your learner carries out safety checks on your vehicle. Developing a habit of regular checks can also help identify faults at an early stage and this may prevent the vehicle breaking down during a journey.

Allowing your learner to clean the windscreen, windows, mirrors and lights will help you and will also help them to remember these aspects.

What to expect

Many new drivers do not have an interest in the workings of the car but they do need to understand

- daily and weekly vehicle checks
- service intervals
- MOT requirements.

The importance of having your vehicle regularly serviced should be stressed and you could show your learner how you keep a record of your car's service intervals.

Remember, 'POWER' –

P   **Petrol**
O   **Oil (engine oil and brake fluid)**
W   **Water (engine coolant, windscreen washers)**
E   **Electrics (lights, indicators)**
R   **Rubber and brakes.**

Controls and instruments

Refer to · p28

Reading and understanding instruments such as the speedometer, fuel and temperature gauge are essential.

By the time your learner is ready for their test they should also understand the warning lamps and, importantly, know what action to take if one comes on while they are driving.

In the early days of learning to drive, controlling the steering, gears and foot controls will take all your learner's concentration. As their skill develops it's also important for them to become competent with ancillary controls such as the demister, wipers, heaters, etc.

How you can help

Allow your learner to familiarise themselves with the layout of the controls and instruments and explain any special features that may be fitted to your car.

The controls may be laid out differently in the ADI's car and this could lead to some confusion; for example, if the windscreen wiper controls are on the left of the steering column instead of on the right.

What to expect

When you're in situations that call for the use of certain controls such as the front or rear screen demister, your learner may be concentrating really hard on their driving and fail to realise the need to use them.

Don't allow the situation to become dangerous, but do encourage your learner to recognise for themselves when these controls should be used.

If your learner fumbles while trying to find and operate the control they want, pull up somewhere safe and run through the control layout again.

> **Remember,** your learner should be able to operate all the controls without looking down to find them.

Moving away and stopping

 Refer to p30

Choosing a safe place to stop and stopping safely are things that every driver needs to do. Your learner will also need to develop sound judgement and awareness of other road users.

How you can help

While your learner is having to concentrate really hard on using the controls, they may forget to watch for other road users. Stay alert and don't let them move off into danger. Practise moving off

- on level ground
- uphill
- downhill
- from behind a parked vehicle.

Asking your learner to pick somewhere safe to stop will allow them to think for themselves. They need to look for somewhere to stop and then use their mirrors and signals correctly while bringing the car to rest at their chosen place.

What to expect

Every time your learner moves off, expect them to go through a lengthy process of finding the biting point and balancing the accelerator and clutch against the handbrake. This will make moving off a slow process and this in turn makes dealing with road junctions more difficult.

Frustration may set in as

- traffic builds up behind
- your learner can't pull out into a space which you would find safe as a driver.

If you find your learner has difficulty with busy junctions, avoid them and pick quieter alternatives until the necessary control skills have developed.

When stopping, watch that your learner doesn't try to stop suddenly without allowing time for using the mirror and signalling if necessary. Use the extra rear view mirror to check the traffic behind you.

Remember, traffic lights are one place where tension can build. When the red light changes it's not uncommon for novices to stall in their rush to move off promptly. This can lead to panic, especially if there's a queue of traffic behind. Stay calm and don't react to another driver sounding their horn – they may not be able to see the L-plates if they're not immediately behind.

Safe positioning

(Refer to   p32)

With experience, judging the car's position becomes second nature, but learning to position accurately is a surprisingly difficult skill to learn.

Some learners look just in front of the car rather than well ahead. This makes it more difficult to judge the car's width and position on the road. As well as the control skills, your learner will need to know

- where to position the car for any particular driving situation
- the meaning of signs and road markings.

How you can help

The skill of being able to judge the car's position on the road from the passenger seat will develop with practice. You may need to reach across and steer into the correct position. Try to remain calm and don't allow the wrong road position to go uncorrected for any length of time.

At first, avoid using places such as narrow streets or roads with width restrictions until your learner has developed a little in both confidence and skill. Then you can move them onto areas and roads requiring more accurate judgement.

What to expect

Before your learner's judgement has developed they may

- drive too close to the kerb, the edge or centre of the road, parked cars, or other obstructions
- position the vehicle poorly around bends and junctions
- show poor lane discipline.

Don't allow your learner to hit the kerb while driving normally. The impact may wrench the steering wheel from their grasp, causing serious loss of control. It may also damage or burst the tyre.

Some mistakes can be scary for you as a passenger but your learner may be unaware of this, or that they have made an error. If it's going wrong, pull over and talk about it. You may need to demonstrate their mistake in order for the learner to realise it for themselves. If you disagree on positioning, then discuss it with the ADI.

Mirrors – vision and use

Refer to   p34

The ADI will cover this subject early in the learning process but watch for your learner having to make exaggerated head movements to use the mirrors. This may mean adjustments are needed, once you have stopped in a safe place.

Correctly adjusted mirrors give a good view behind and to the sides of the car. It's important that your learner uses the mirrors when necessary and is aware of the areas not covered by the mirrors (and that they know how and when to check them).

How you can help

When accompanying your learner, look to see if they are checking mirrors correctly. If a mirror check is missed you should always draw their attention to it but avoid prompting them too early – they may become reliant on your prompt rather than thinking for themselves.

Don't let them change direction without first checking that it is safe.

To check if your learner is using their mirrors, fit another small interior mirror on the left of the windscreen, angled so that you can see your learner without having to look directly at them.

> **Remember,** when turning right in busy traffic there will be occasions when a blind area check to the right needs to be made in case a vehicle is attempting to overtake. There may be so much else going on that this check is missed and you may need to make it on their behalf.

What to expect

When watching your learner's use of mirrors check

- how well they time their mirror checks
- that they act correctly on what can be seen.

You may find yourself having to look and plan further ahead than normal, so that you can identify hazards early enough to then be watching to see how your learner deals with them. This can have an extra benefit in that it improves your own hazard awareness.

Signals

Refer to   p36

Drivers need to know how and when to give signals and the meaning of signals given by others. Whichever way signals are given, they must be given clearly and in good time. Your learner must be able to identify the signals of others and act correctly on them.

How you can help

Watch your learner's use of signals and make sure they use only signals shown in *The Official Highway Code*. Try to use routes which will expose your learner to the need to think about the timing of a signal or whether a signal is appropriate; for example

- when passing a parked car with a road junction on the right

- turning right or left when there is another junction just before your turn.

If in any doubt about the correct procedure, ask the ADI for advice.

What to expect

In the early part of their training, learners will be thinking about their use of the car controls and may forget to signal. This may be dangerous, for example, when pulling up while being followed by another vehicle. Remain alert and give help in good time if safety is threatened.

There may be occasions where another road user gives a signal that your learner hasn't met before, such as reversing lights on a car that is trying to reverse park into a space on the side of the road.

Learners tend to shy away from using the horn. However, it is a valuable aid to road safety when used correctly and you should encourage its use when appropriate.

Most indicators will automatically cancel after a manoeuvre but they may not. Don't let an uncancelled signal continue for any length of time – it could mislead another road user and lead to danger.

> **Remember,** the horn must only be used while the vehicle is moving, to make other road users aware of your presence. Refer your learner to *The Official Highway Code*.

Anticipation and planning

Refer to p38

Before your learner can react to a risk they must perceive that a risk exists. That perception is governed by

- training (in this situation do this)
- experience (I've met this before and need to do this)
- planning (what should I do now to prevent risk in the situation I can see?)
- anticipation (what if?).

One of the main problems for inexperienced drivers is that they don't recognise the hazard until it is too late to avoid the danger.

How you can help

Practice is so important. During practice, your learner will meet situations that they have never met before. While you are sitting next to them, your experience in both seeing and reacting to any risk should keep them safe and, where possible, you can pass on the benefit of your experience.

Whilst your learner can never experience every type of hazard, you can aim to instil in them a heightened awareness of hazards and a knowledge of how to cope with them.

What to expect

Your learner may feel they have everything under control, but if the way they deal with hazards makes you feel uncomfortable, something is wrong with their driving. When a mistake has been made you'll need to highlight the potential danger in their response to a situation.

Learners can be defensive about their driving ability and you should take account of their feelings. Stay calm and don't raise your voice, but do make sure they understand the consequences of their actions.

Remember, new drivers often don't look very far ahead. They can be too slow to identify potential danger and don't realise how soon they need to react.

Step in to help before danger develops.

Use of speed

Refer to   p40

Driving too fast is one of the main causes of road accidents on all types of roads. Driving too slowly is a different mistake and one that creates its own set of hazards.

So how fast should your learner be driving? What is a suitable speed? The answer is dependent on a number of variables and getting it right takes practice.

Your learner must never drive beyond their ability or the speed limit but they will need to reach a level of being able to drive on all roads without hindering the flow of traffic.

How you can help

The more practice your learner can have of various driving situations, the better they'll become at assessing the correct speed to suit different conditions and reacting to changes in the speed limit.

If your learner is timid, remember that they may take a long time to feel confident with making progress.

If you think your learner is not improving very quickly, don't be negative or critical – a timid driver needs encouragement, not criticism. Learning to drive is a lengthy process so you'll need to allow more time for more practice.

Don't ignore rural roads where wide variations in speed can be experienced, as this will be good practice for your learner. In these rural areas they will have to

- plan ahead
- continually adjust their speed.

Remember, make sure your learner obeys speed limits and understands that they're not targets – they are the maximum speed legally permitted.
It is not always safe to drive up to the speed limit.

What to expect

You can expect your learner to start by driving slowly in all situations. In particular, expect very slow acceleration up through the gears, which can make emerging at junctions difficult and, for you, frustrating.

For the first few practice sessions, don't let your learner drive the car if you are in a hurry to get somewhere as this may make you feel impatient.

If you become critical and negative, what sort of message do you think this gives your learner about correct driver behaviour towards other road users?

You need to be patient, tolerant and understanding. As experience and confidence grow, speeds will increase and skills in hazard awareness and planning ahead will develop. However, overconfidence and an irresponsible attitude towards risk need to be discouraged.

The ADI will teach your learner how to keep a safe distance from the vehicle in front, but they must then put this theory into practice when they drive. Help them practise applying the two-second rule appropriately and safely until it becomes a habit.

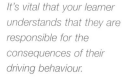

It's vital that your learner understands that they are responsible for the consequences of their driving behaviour.

Other traffic

Refer to   p42

Your learner needs to gain experience of dealing with traffic while having the safety net of an experienced driver sitting by their side. Whilst you can't cover every possible situation, you should be able to help them learn to deal safely with

- meeting oncoming traffic
- turning across the path of other vehicles
- overtaking
- parked vehicles or other obstructions.

How you can help

These traffic situations call for judgement and often there is little or no room for error. Don't allow your learner to overestimate their own ability or their car's performance. If they make a mistake you're there to prevent it from developing into something more serious.

Avoid busy main roads until confidence has developed. Find places to practise that include

- narrow roads
- parked cars and other obstructions
- roads with right-turn lane markings
- traffic lights
- box junctions.

As well as practising dealing with obstructions on your side of the road, find places where your learner has to anticipate the actions of an approaching driver who might not give way. For hazards that you don't encounter you can always talk to your learner about possible situations. Thinking about potential danger is a big part of developing hazard awareness.

> **Remember,** you're responsible for ensuring that your learner doesn't create dangerous situations through inexperience or lack of judgement.

What to expect

Learners will usually be cautious – on busy roads you may wait for some time. Don't become frustrated if you feel that some opportunities are being missed – as confidence builds, so will ability.

When waiting to turn right, you may find oncoming drivers will give way and invite your learner to complete turning. Before accepting, your learner must check for other road users, such as motorcyclists and cyclists. When overtaking, many mistakes can be made through inexperience and lack of judgement.

Errors can include

- overtaking too slowly
- overtaking when the vehicle in front is driving close to the speed limit
- not allowing enough room
- cutting in too soon after overtaking.

Also remember that, if your car is different from the ADI's, your learner may also take time to get used to judging its width.

When meeting oncoming traffic, your learner needs to judge the available space and, if necessary, give way.

Junctions

Refer to   p44

Dealing with junctions includes driving straight ahead as well as turning right and left. They can be any shape or size, including those with

- road markings
- no road markings
- traffic lights
- warning signs.

Your learner will have to learn where and when they should be looking and what they are looking for. Interpreting what they see and planning how to deal with the possible outcomes is a skill which develops with experience.

Whilst your learner should already be familiar with the signs and markings in *The Official Highway Code*, they first have to see the sign or marking and realise how it affects them before acting on the information given.

> **Remember,** don't be fooled by your learner's apparent confidence – their hazard perception skills will not be well-developed even though they think they are observing well and feel everything is under control.

It's important to explain the importance of assessing whether another road user has seen you when dealing with junctions – it may take a while for them develop this ability.

Correctly timed signals help other road users to know your learner's intentions.

How you can help

Refer to the *Driver's Record* to see what level your learner has reached and plan their practice accordingly.

Try to find junctions where you can practise turning into as well as out of side roads, or one where your learner can drive round a circuit or block.

When planning a location, consider whether

- there will be much traffic
- both turns and emerges can be practised
- there are road markings to help with · positioning
- there are any difficulties, for example, steep slopes or poor visibility at any of the junctions.

What to expect

The ADI will already have covered the Mirror–Signal–Manoeuvre routine for dealing with junctions. However, new learners may be struggling with steering or changing gear while trying to think about speed, mirrors, road position and signs.

> **Remember,** if your learner is not confident in their ability to move off, they may try to emerge from a junction without stopping to see if it's safe. If you can't see that it's safe, neither can they.
>
> **Don't let them cause an accident.**

In addition, new drivers often don't look very far ahead and may not see, or may misjudge, any approaching traffic. They can also be slow to identify potential danger.

Mistakes can easily happen and a mistake at a junction can be dangerous as well as frightening for both of you. If you can't see that it's safe, then neither can your learner. Keep calm and step in to help before any danger develops.

Roundabouts

Refer to | p46

Many learners find it difficult to cope with roundabouts. The ADI may ask for them to be practised in stages, eg turning left, turning right and going ahead. If that's the case, you'll need to plan routes accordingly.

Try to include a variety, from large multi-lane roundabouts to small and mini-roundabouts.

> **Remember,** rear-end collisions are very common at roundabouts, often caused when a driver waiting to join one doesn't do so and the driver behind expects them to move. The driver behind then moves forward while looking for traffic on the roundabout and not checking if the car in front has continued to move forward. Be aware of this hazard at busy roundabouts.

How you can help

When you're approaching a roundabout tell your learner which direction you want them to go in plenty of time. If possible, use other instructions to help them, such as 'follow the sign to the town centre' or 'the third exit'.

If your learner becomes disorientated, tell them in good time where their exit is, to allow them time to position correctly.

If they miss the exit, don't worry. Direct them round again, using the appropriate lane or road position and take the exit required. You need to encourage your learner to plan their route onto, around and off the roundabout. Try to avoid a situation where your learner is part-way around the roundabout before they start to think about which road they should be taking.

What to expect

If your learner is uncertain of the direction they are supposed to be taking, expect incorrect signalling and positioning. They may also

- drive too slowly, which can cause problems if there's fast-moving traffic

- veer suddenly to take an exit at the last moment with no thought for other traffic.

Learners often struggle with directions on roundabouts. Try to get them to make use of the signs so that they know what to expect.

Dual carriageways

Refer to p48

Dual carriageways aren't governed by the same regulations that apply on motorways.

Driving at higher speeds and in lanes on a dual carriageway gives valuable experience both in itself and in preparation for motorway driving once the driving test has been passed.

How you can help

As well as driving in the correct lane along the carriageway, your learner needs to gain experience of

- using slip roads
- turning right
- overtaking
- high-speed traffic.

Gaining such experience during adverse weather conditions, in twilight and during the hours of darkness is also very valuable.

What to expect

Most learners begin by driving relatively slowly and this is fine when driving along a dual carriageway. However, joining a dual carriageway from a slip road can call for firm acceleration. If your learner is not too confident with accelerating through the gears, wait until the skill has developed before attempting to join a dual carriageway.

When overtaking, your learner will need to judge the length of their vehicle accurately. If they don't, there's a danger of cutting in too soon as they return to the left lane.

Remember, vehicles ahead may want to turn right through the central reservation. Don't let your learner confuse their right signal and positioning in the right lane as a sign that they are overtaking when other clues (such as brake lights or a junction sign) show that they may be turning right.

Pedestrian crossings

Refer to   p50

There are laws governing pedestrian crossings which your learner must know and with which they must comply. There are also several types of pedestrian crossing – do you know them all?

How you can help

When your learner is approaching a crossing, see if they can tell you what type of crossing it is and what rules apply.

Going out for a drive at school start and finish times should ensure plenty of opportunities to deal with busy crossings.

Darkness adds another aspect to safely dealing with pedestrian crossings, and practice during twilight or the hours of darkness is recommended.

What to expect

Noticing there's a crossing ahead is the first hurdle. You'll soon tell if your learner hasn't and you may need to act promptly. Don't let your learner over-react and stop unnecessarily. This could cause a danger to traffic behind you.

Make certain they understand the sequence of lights at light-controlled crossings, and react correctly to each phase of the lights.

Remember, pedestrians are among the most vulnerable road users. If you have any doubts about your learner's ability to cope, give assistance until you're happy that they can cope unaided and without any risk of losing control.

Turning the vehicle around

Refer to — **p52**

The skills needed to turn the car around in the road will be needed every time your learner has to manoeuvre in a confined space.

How you can help

You may wish to familiarise yourself with the technique taught by the ADI. This is explained in detail in *The Official DSA Guide to Driving – the essential skills.* When looking for a place to practise the exercise, consider

- road width
- visibility
- traffic volume
- local residents.

Be courteous to other road users while your learner is practising. Be prepared to find somewhere else if the first place turns out to be less suitable than you first thought.

What to expect

Some learners can take time to recall techniques they've been taught – panic may set in and disorientation may follow half-way through an exercise. They might struggle with the controls, fail to notice other road users or be unable to judge the car's length.

Be supportive and offer encouragement rather than criticism if it's all taking longer than you anticipated.

> **Remember,** a sudden loss of control when turning can cause surging forward or backwards onto the pavement and colliding with whatever is in the way. You'll need to act promptly if your learner loses control in this manner.

Turn to the right and then briskly to the left just before you stop.

Turn to the left and then briskly to the right just before you stop.

Straighten up and make sure that you stay on your side of the road.

Reversing

For many learners, reversing accurately is the most difficult part of learning to drive. Statistics show this is a key reason for learners failing the driving test.

If your learner finds reversing difficult, you can expect to spend a lot of time practising this skill.

How you can help

It's easier to begin by practising reversing into a junction on the left rather than on the right. The techniques for both are described in *The Official DSA Guide to Driving – the essential skills.*

Look for a place to practise where

* there's good visibility
* the road is level
* you don't expect much traffic
* you won't annoy local residents.

A crossroads or staggered junction is not a suitable location to practise reversing. Don't just use one location but try to find a variety of junctions for practice sessions.

What to expect

Reversing doesn't come easily to many learners. If your learner becomes despondent, move on to another topic and return to reversing practice another day.

Practising on an uphill slope before skills have developed is likely to cause wear on the clutch and noise as the engine is excessively revved. Try to avoid this until your learner has developed some skill and confidence in reversing on flat ground.

> **Remember,** good all-round observation is essential when reversing.

Modern cars have an exterior mirror fitted on both sides of the car. If these mirrors are used for reversing remember that

* there is no view directly behind the car
* the driver may focus solely on the detail seen in the mirror and fail to see other road users or obstructions
* the mirrors are not set for rear observation when driving.

Parking

Refer to   p56

On the driving test your learner may be asked to demonstrate their ability to park by reversing into a parking bay in a car park or a space behind another parked car on the side of the road. The ADI will have taught the procedures as explained in *The Official DSA Guide to Driving – the essential skills*.

> **Remember,** whether parking in a car park or on the roadside, your learner should be able to position the car accurately, confidently and safely. You must ensure that your learner doesn't hit another vehicle while practising.

How you can help

When practising reverse parking on the side of the road, your learner will inevitably cause a temporary obstruction to any traffic flow. For this reason, choose a quiet location for practice.

To practise reversing into a parking bay, you will need to find a suitable car park where your learner can practise this manoeuvre. Avoid busy car parks and peak times of day. Try to find a parking bay that has an empty bay on either side, which will allow a greater margin for inaccurate steering. While your learner's vehicle control skills are developing, you can help by being their eyes and ears watching out for other road users. As car control develops, you can let them become responsible for the safety aspects themselves.

As with other reverse manoeuvres, don't allow your learner to rely only on the car's mirrors while reversing.

What to expect

Reverse parking calls for accuracy, control and judgement. Your learner may be weak on any or all of these skills. When they set about reverse parking on the side of the road, you can expect them to have trouble judging where to pull up in readiness to reverse into the space. This may result in pulling up too close alongside, or too far past, the parked car, or perhaps not far enough forward past the parking space.

If your learner misjudges the car's length when reversing into a parking bay, they may go beyond the edge of the bay, or into a wall or barrier, causing damage to your car.

To park on the roadside, your learner should pull up reasonably close to and parallel with the vehicle in front.

Make sure your learner doesn't hit the parked vehicle and is aware of passing traffic.

The car should be parked within the space of about two car lengths, close to and parallel with the kerb.

Emergency stop

Refer to   p58

Practising stopping the car as if there was an emergency provides valuable experience in reacting quickly and correctly while controlling the car under emergency conditions. Practising what to do in an emergency is the only way to help your learner to cope if a real situation ever arises.

> **Remember,** relying on your additional interior mirror to tell you what's behind isn't enough.

How you can help

Find somewhere with very little traffic, a good road surface, and where screeching tyres won't cause a nuisance. Agree with your learner the signal to give and begin practising at low speeds. Only progress to higher speeds when your learner has gained sufficient control skills to cope. Also, make sure you look around carefully before giving any signal to stop.

What to expect

The ADI will have given instruction in use of the controls. If your vehicle has an anti-lock braking system fitted, there may be special instructions on how to achieve maximum braking. Be prepared for your learner to use excessive force when applying the brakes which may cause

- skidding accompanied by loud screeching and smoke from the tyres
- a severe jolt which could cause injury to your back or neck.

On giving the signal, brace yourself and prepare for a sudden rapid deceleration.

Independent driving

Refer to **p60**

Learning to drive independently is an important part of preparing your learner

- for their driving test
- to drive after they have passed their driving test.

Learner drivers can come to rely on the direction they are given as a prompt to begin the MSM-PSL routine. By removing the step-by-step directions, they will need to think for themselves and plan ahead, exactly as they will when driving unaccompanied.

> **Remember,** your learner may forget the directions and you will need to help, but if they wait until they have arrived at a junction before asking, they haven't planned ahead.

How you can help

To help your learner drive independently you will need to give them some very simple directions. These may be to follow directions shown by road signs or a short series of two or three right and left turns.

Keep it as simple as you can so that remembering the directions isn't difficult.

What to expect

At first they may be so focused thinking about the directions that they forget to signal or are late moving into the correct lane or road position. They may also overlook other important features such as traffic lights, pedestrian crossings or road markings and you should be ready to step in if necessary. Once they start to think for themselves and plan ahead they will be better prepared for driving after their test.

Darkness

Refer to   p62

Your learner needs to practise driving in the dark since this calls for a new set of skills. As well as knowing how and when to use the car's lights, they have to learn how to cope with

- poor visibility when light levels are low
- glare from the lights of other vehicles
- not dazzling other road users.

How you can help

Try to give your learner as much experience as possible of driving in the dark in a range of areas such as well-lit urban roads, unlit rural roads and dual carriageways. When driving in the dark, show your learner

- how to use the anti-dazzle mirror, if your car has one fitted
- how and when to dip the main beam headlights to avoid dazzling others.

When driving on rural roads without footpaths, ask them to think about pedestrians.

- Where should they be walking?
- What if they are wearing dark clothing?

Could your learner cope?

Make sure they check *The Official Highway Code* for advice and rules on driving, parking, vehicle lighting and use of the horn at night.

What to expect

The bright lights of oncoming traffic can be difficult to cope with. If an approaching driver has forgotten to dip their headlights, your learner may be dazzled and unable to see the road ahead. Don't let them

- continue without reducing speed
- retaliate by using their headlights to dazzle the approaching driver.

Don't forget that vulnerable road users like cyclists, pedestrians and motorcyclists may be very difficult to see in the dark.

Many people adapt easily to driving in the dark – others find it very tiring. If your learner finds it tiring, be ready to end the practice session and take over the driving yourself.

> **Remember,** in busy urban areas, lights from shops and street lamps can make it easy to miss traffic lights, crossing lights, vulnerable road users, etc. You're responsible for making sure no mistakes are made.

Weather conditions

Refer to p64

Adverse weather conditions such as fog, frost, high winds and rain are all common driving conditions.

In more severe weather conditions of snow and ice, be guided by the advice of local travel experts to determine whether conditions are suitable for your learner.

How you can help

If the conditions aren't severe, you should take opportunities for your learner to practise when possible. In bad weather your learner needs to pay attention to how the conditions affect their

- speed and ability to stop
- use of windscreen wipers/demisters
- need to use dipped headlights.

Explain that, just because they may think they can see adequately during the day in dull, foggy or wet conditions, this does not mean their vehicle can be seen clearly by others. If in doubt, use sidelights for safety and visibility until conditions improve.

What to expect

Driving too close to the vehicle in front is a common mistake. Make sure the two-second rule is used, and that the gap is increased if conditions will affect the stopping distance. If fitted, front or rear fog lights may be used but make sure they are turned off if conditions improve.

Also remember that anti-lock brakes (ABS) do not replace the need for good driving skill. ABS prevents wheels locking so that steering control is retained, but vehicles can still skid because of factors such as ice, surface water and loose road surface. Make sure your learner fully understands this.

Environmental issues

| Refer to | p66 |

Your learner needs to understand that they can reduce exhaust emissions by driving in an environmentally friendly manner. They will save money by using less fuel, and improve their hazard awareness skills by looking and planning further ahead.

How you can help

The ADI should be able to explain the recommended driving techniques which can also be found in *The Official DSA Guide to Driving – the essential skills*. Encourage your learner to practise these techniques.

Keeping a check on fuel consumption will show you the effect that driving in an environmentally friendly manner can have. This may encourage you to adopt these techniques yourself.

To help your learner appreciate environmental issues other than fuel consumption, talk about

- the importance of good maintenance, and keeping tyres correctly inflated
- disposal of oil, old tyres and batteries.

Remember, harsh use of the accelerator and heavy braking significantly increases fuel consumption.

What to expect

Learners tend to drive more slowly than experienced drivers until their confidence builds. You can help your learner to understand that maintaining careful use of speed and an awareness of fuel consumption will help them continue to drive in an environmentally friendly manner. Encourage them to keep doing so.

Passengers and loads

Refer to p68

Your learner must understand the driver's responsibility when carrying passengers. They must be aware of the latest seat belt requirements according to regulations, details of which are in *The Official Highway Code*.

They must also understand the effect a load can have on a vehicle's handling/braking and the importance of not overloading their vehicle. Help your learner develop good awareness of their responsibilities to prevent them from breaking the law.

How you can help

Letting your learner drive with passengers can be a valuable experience. If any are under 14 years, the driver is responsible for ensuring that they are wearing a seat belt or appropriate child restraint. Make sure your learner is aware of this.

Use any opportunity to let your learner practise in a loaded vehicle, for example when going on holiday. Discuss the way extra weight can affect the vehicle and explain the importance of making sure that the load is secure and not sticking out dangerously.

Refer to the vehicle handbook for advice on altering tyre pressures when carrying heavy loads.

What to expect

If the car is heavily loaded, its acceleration may be slower than normal. Make sure your learner takes this into account when emerging from a side road, or moving off on an uphill gradient. Braking may also be affected – make sure your learner understands this and that they should allow themselves more time and greater distance in which to stop the vehicle safely.

If you're carrying an animal such as a family pet in the car, it's important to keep it under control. Loose animals can be a serious distraction and could cause an accident.

> **Remember,** if the car is filled with people, there's likely to be conversation. Make sure this doesn't distract either of you.

Security

Refer to   p70

Your learner needs to be aware of the importance of security, not only of the vehicle and its contents but also their own personal security. Information on vehicle safety can be obtained from your local Crime Prevention Officer.

How you can help

When looking for a place to park the car, your learner may be preoccupied with the process of parking and not thinking about the security issues.

If they choose to park in a place that has a security risk, ask them if they think they have chosen a safe place to park. If necessary you should point out the risk. Make sure they understand the importance of not parking in poorly lit areas or leaving any valuables on display.

If your vehicle is fitted with an immobiliser and/or alarm, make sure your learner is familiar with its operation and that they use it whenever they park the car.

If you have a high-visibility security device such as a steering wheel lock, show your learner how to use it.

What to expect

If your learner is naturally security-conscious, they will happily take measures that cut down the risks. If not, you may have to nag them to understand that using a car makes them a potential target for car crime; it is in their own interest to safeguard themselves and their property.

Remember, many car crimes are committed on petrol station forecourts when the driver leaves the car to pay for fuel. Alerting your learner to the risk may prevent them from becoming a victim.

section **four**
THE TEST AND BEYOND

This section covers

- Are you ready for your test?
- Booking your practical driving test
- The day of your test
- The practical test
- Your test result
- Pass Plus
- Developing your driving skill

Are you ready for your test?

You'll be ready for your practical test when you show that you've reached **Level 5** in all the key skills listed on the *Driver's Record*, not before.

Those learner drivers who pass first time do so because they've had plenty of professional instruction and practice. About 45% of those taking their practical test actually pass – make sure you're one of them.

> **Remember,** your instructor has the knowledge and experience to tell you when you're ready. You'll be ready when you can drive consistently well, with confidence and without assistance or guidance. If you can't do this all the time, you're not ready to take your test.

Are you sure you're ready to drive on your own? – Don't put in for your test too soon; wait until you're ready. It'll save you time and money.

It's important that throughout your training you've been learning the theory and putting this into practice when you drive – you need to do the two things in parallel. However, you do need to take and pass a theory test before you can apply to take your practical driving test.

The theory test

There are two parts to the theory test: the first consisting of multiple choice questions, the second a hazard perception part. Both are taken in the same session.

There are over 150 theory test centres in Great Britain and Northern Ireland. Theory test sessions are available during weekdays, evenings and on Saturdays.

It's important that you study, not just to pass the test, but to become a safer driver.

You'll usually be able to get an appointment within about two weeks (a bit longer if you have special needs).

You can find out where your local centre is from your instructor, online at **direct.gov.uk/motoringnearest** or by calling **0300 200 1122.** More information about the theory test and the multiple choice questions is given in *The Official DSA Theory Test for Car Drivers* book or CD-ROM.

The Official DSA Guide to Hazard Perception DVD will help you prepare for the hazard perception part of the theory test as well as preparing you for driving on the road.

When you pass your theory test you'll be given a pass certificate. You have to quote the number when you book your practical test and you must bring the certificate with you when you take your practical test.

The theory test certificate is valid for two years. If you don't pass your practical test within that time, you'll have to take and pass another theory test before you can book your practical test.

When you drive on your practical test, your examiner will expect you to demonstrate what you've learnt for your theory test.

I can't read English very well, so I'm a bit worried about taking my theory test.

You can listen to the test being read out in one of 20 languages, or you can take a translator with you to certain centres. If you have reading difficulties or dyslexia there's also an English language voiceover and you may be allowed extra time in some circumstances – don't forget to enquire about this when you're booking.

How will I know what to do on the hazard perception part of the test?

Once you've done the multiple choice part of the test, and before you start the hazard perception part, you'll be shown a short tutorial video that explains how the test works and gives you a chance to see a sample film clip. This will help you to understand what you're expected to do once the second part of the test starts.

Booking your practical driving test

How to book

You have all the **Level 5** boxes on your *Driver's Record* completed, you've passed your theory test and are ready to take your practical test.

It's easiest to book your test online or by telephone, but you can also book by post.

Online or by telephone – If you book by either of these methods, you'll be given the date and time of your test immediately. You can book online at **direct.gov.uk/drivingtest**

To book by telephone, call **0300 200 1122** Monday to Friday. If you're deaf and use a minicom machine, call **0300 200 1144** and if you're a Welsh speaker, call **0300 200 1133.**

You'll need to tell them what sort of test you want to book and provide

- your theory test pass certificate number
- your driver number shown on your licence
- your driving school code number (if you have it)
- your credit/debit card details. Please note that the person who books the test must be the card holder.

You may be asked if you can accept a test at short notice. Ask your instructor beforehand about this if you would need to use their car. You'll be given a booking number and sent an appointment letter within a few days.

Booking by post – Fill in an application form which you can get from driving test centres or your instructor. Send the form, together with the correct fee, to the address shown on the back of the form. Don't forget to give your preferred date when you book.

You may pay by cheque, postal order or with a credit/debit card. Please don't send cash. You'll receive an appointment letter within 10 days.

Apply well in advance of when you want to take your test. At test centres in Wales, you can take the test in the Welsh language. Please indicate your choice when booking.

You'll receive an appointment letter which will include the time and place of your test, the address of the driving test centre and other important information. If you haven't received one after two weeks, call **0300 200 1122**.

Disabilities or special circumstances

Whichever way you book your test, you need to let them know when booking if you have a disability or if there are other special circumstances. However serious your disability is, you will still take the same driving test as every other test candidate but more time is allowed for the test.

This is so that your examiner can talk to you about your disability and any adaptations fitted to your vehicle. For further information, please see the list of useful addresses on page 3.

To make sure that enough time is allowed for your test, it would help DSA to know if you

- are deaf or have severe hearing difficulties
- are in any way restricted in your movements
- have any disability which may affect your driving.

If any of these apply to you, please say so when you book your test. If you can't speak English or are deaf, you are allowed to bring an interpreter (this can be your instructor). The interpreter must be 16 years or over.

How much does the test cost?

Your instructor should be able to tell you or you can find out on direct.gov.uk/motoring or by calling **0300 200 1122**.

Can I take my test at a weekend or in the evening?

At some test centres you can take a test on a Saturday, Sunday or weekday evening. The fees at these times are higher than for tests during normal working hours on weekdays. Evening tests are available during the summer months only.

How do I change or cancel my test?

You can change or cancel your test online at direct.gov.uk/drivingtest or by calling the booking office on **0300 200 1122** (you may even be able to switch to an earlier date).

You must give at least three clear working days' notice, not counting the day DSA received your request and the day of the test (Saturday is counted as a working day). If you don't give enough notice, you'll lose your fee.

The day of your test

Make sure that you arrive for your test in good time and try to relax. You need to bring the correct documents with you and ensure that the vehicle you'll be driving is suitable to take out on test.

Before your test, you will have to sign a declaration that your insurance is in order and that you meet the residency requirements.

Documents

When you arrive at the test centre you need to have with you

- your provisional driving licence – if you have a photocard licence you must bring both parts with you
- your theory test pass certificate
- your valid passport, if your licence doesn't show your photograph (your passport doesn't have to be British). No other form of identification is acceptable except in Northern Ireland; please check **dvani.gov.uk**

Don't forget, if you have completed a *Driver's Record*, bring this with you as well. Any of the following licences are acceptable

- a provisional driving licence issued in Great Britain or Northern Ireland, or a full GB or NI licence giving the provisional entitlement
- an EC/EEA licence accompanied by a GB licence counterpart, if you want to take a test for a category not covered by your full EU licence.

If you have a full driving licence which was issued in another country but isn't eligible for exchange for a GB licence, you must have a GB provisional licence. Your examiner will not be able to conduct the test if you can't produce one of these licences.

All documents must be original – DSA can't accept photocopies.

Your test vehicle

Make sure that the vehicle you're going to drive during the test is

- legally roadworthy and has a current MOT test certificate if it needs one
- mechanically sound and all equipment required by law must be fitted and working correctly; for example, the speedometer must show mph and km/h. In some cars the spare wheel is a space-saver intended for temporary use only. You can't take your test if one of these is in use

117

- fully covered by insurance for its present use and for you to drive – your examiner will ask you to sign a declaration that your insurance is in order before you take your test.

A hire car is unlikely to be insured for the driving test. You should check with the hire company when you hire the car.

The vehicle should also have

- a valid tax disc displayed
- L plates (or, if you wish, D plates, if taking your test in Wales) displayed to the front and rear of the vehicle – don't fix them to the windscreen or back window as both you and your examiner should have a clear view of the road
- seat belts – make sure they're clean and work properly

Can I take my test in an automatic car?

You can, but if you pass you'll only get a full licence to drive an automatic. There is sometimes some confusion about what is classed as an automatic, but for driving test purposes only vehicles with three pedals (accelerator, brake and clutch) are classed as manual; vehicles with two pedals are classed as automatics.

- head restraints fitted ('slip-on' type head restraints are not permissible on test)
- an additional interior rear-view mirror for the examiner to use.

Remember, if you overlook any of these points your test will be cancelled and you'll lose your fee. Make sure your vehicle is suitable for the test well in advance.

The controls, seating, equipment and any other objects in the vehicle must be arranged so that they don't interfere with the conduct of the test. A dual accelerator (if fitted) must be removed before the test.

You won't be able to take your test if your vehicle isn't suitable; for example, if it

- has no clear view to the rear – other than by use of the exterior mirrors
- has only a driver's seat
- has more than eight passenger seats or is over 3.5 tonnes in weight
- doesn't have seat belts or head restraints fitted to the front passenger seat
- has been subject to a manufacturer's recall but you don't have a certificate showing that the work has been carried out
- is loaded or partly loaded
- is towing a trailer (see page 129).

If you are using a left-hand drive car, take special care and make full use of your mirrors.

The practical test

You should aim to reach **Level 5** in all the key skills. Try to relax and drive as you've been driving during your lessons and practice.

Your examiner wants you to do well and will try to help you relax. If you want to talk during the test, that won't be a problem – your examiner will talk with you but might not say too much because they don't want to distract you from your driving. Don't worry if you make a mistake, keep calm and concentrate on your driving for the rest of the test. Unless it is a serious or dangerous fault you won't fail on this unless you make the same mistake a number of times.

You'll pass if you can show your examiner that you can drive safely and demonstrate, through your driving, that you have a thorough knowledge of the rules of *The Official Highway Code* and the theory of driving safely.

Does the standard of test vary?

No, all examiners are trained to assess tests to the same standard. The test routes are designed to include a range of typical road and traffic conditions and the examiners are closely supervised to make sure they follow the national standard. A senior examiner sits in on some tests to make sure the examiner is assessing the standard of your driving properly. If this happens on your test, don't worry – they won't be looking at you, so just carry on as if they weren't there.

Can anyone accompany me on the test?

Yes, we encourage this. The examiner will ask you if you would like your instructor, or anyone else (preferably the person who trained you to drive) to accompany you on test and be there for the result and end-of-test feedback.

It can be helpful to take your instructor with you. Pass or fail, your instructor can discuss your test with you and identify any further training you might need.

Anyone who goes with you must be 16 or over and wear a seat belt, but they must not take any part in the test.

If you need an interpreter you can bring one with you. If appropriate, your instructor may also act as interpreter during your test.

Your driving instructor should be preparing you to drive alone after you have passed the test, so you should already be learning the skills you need to do so and to make decisions for yourself. Once you have passed your test you will need to navigate roads safely, often dealing with other distractions such as passengers and music.

Throughout the test your examiner will be watching how you drive and how you put into practice the things you've learnt for your theory test.

You must satisfy them that you have fully understood all aspects, especially

- alertness and concentration
- courtesy and consideration
- care in the use of the controls to reduce mechanical wear and tear
- awareness of stopping distances, speed limits and safety margins in all conditions
- hazard awareness
- correct action concerning pedestrians and other vulnerable road users
- dealing with other types of vehicle in the correct manner
- road and traffic signs.

The test lasts for about 40 minutes. The route has been selected to include as many different road and traffic conditions as possible.

Your examiner will give you directions clearly and in good time, but if you're not sure about anything just ask. Your examiner understands that you might be nervous and won't mind explaining again.

Other elements in the test

Apart from general driving, your test will include the following:

Eyesight test – before you get into your car your examiner will point out a vehicle at a suitable distance and ask you to read its number plate. You must satisfy them that you can read it as detailed on page 10. If you need glasses or contact lenses to read the number plate, that's fine, but you must wear them during the test and whenever you drive.

If you can't speak English or have difficulty reading, you may copy down what you see.

If your answer is incorrect, your examiner will measure the exact distance and repeat the test. If you fail the eyesight test, your test will go no further.

Safety checks – your examiner will ask you two questions about carrying out safety checks on your vehicle before the start of your test (see page 26).

Special exercises – you'll be asked to carry out one of the following exercises during your test

- reversing around a corner
- turning in the road
- reverse parking (either in a bay at the test centre or on the side of the road).

The exercise will be randomly chosen by your examiner so you should be prepared to demonstrate any one of them. Your examiner will ask you to pull up, explain the exercise and ask you to carry it out.

Independent driving – all practical driving tests will include approximately 10 minutes of independent driving, during which you will be asked to drive by

- following traffic signs to a destination, **or**
- following a series of verbal directions, **or**
- following a combination of both.

This part of the test will enable your examiner to assess how you manage traffic and road systems on your own, and show that you have the skills to be a safe novice driver.

For further information on this part of the test please check the latest details at **direct.gov.uk/motoring**

Your examiner will also ask you to pull up on the left several times during the test. This is to demonstrate your ability to stop and move away

- safely
- while in full control of your car.

Emergency stop – you may be asked to carry out an emergency stop (one in three tests include an emergency stop exercise).

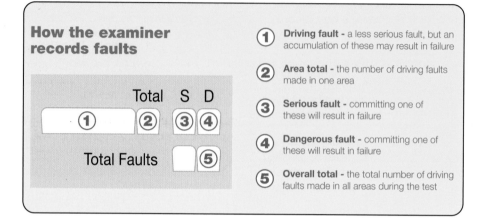

How the examiner records faults

Total S D

① ② ③④

Total Faults ⑤

① **Driving fault -** a less serious fault, but an accumulation of these may result in failure

② **Area total -** the number of driving faults made in one area

③ **Serious fault -** committing one of these will result in failure

④ **Dangerous fault -** committing one of these will result in failure

⑤ **Overall total -** the total number of driving faults made in all areas during the test

How your driving test is assessed

Your examiner is looking for evidence that you have the required skills, knowledge and attitude to be a safe driver.

Throughout your driving test, your examiner will assess your driving and will complete a Driving Test Report which is used to provide you with feedback at the end of the test.

You'll fail your test if you commit a serious or dangerous fault. You'll also fail if you commit more than 15 driving faults.

The examiner will use the following criteria

Driving fault – Less serious, but has been assessed as such because of circumstances at that particular time. An accumulation of more than 15 driving faults will result in failure.

Serious fault – Recorded when a potentially dangerous incident has occurred or a habitual driving fault indicates a serious weakness in a candidate's driving.

Dangerous fault – Recorded when a fault is assessed as having caused actual danger during the test.

Guidance after the test

After the test, pass or fail, you'll be offered feedback on your driving performance and an explanation of your Driving Test Report.

The Data Protection Act prevents your instructor from talking to your examiner about your practical test without your permission.

Having your instructor in the car will give them the opportunity to support your ongoing learning and development. We encourage you to let your instructor see your test and listen to the test result and feedback.

If you have not passed, your instructor will have a better understanding of the reasons for this and they can then address the specific weaknesses you have shown during the drive through further training before your next test.

If you have passed, your instructor will be better placed to advise you about your ongoing development as a new driver.

Ecosafe driving

Ecosafe driving is a recognised and proven style of driving that contributes to road safety whilst reducing fuel consumption and emissions.

At the end of the test, the examiner will debrief you on your ecosafe driving performance and also provide a leaflet that gives further information to help you develop your skills.

Your test result

If you don't pass

Your driving isn't up to the standard required. You made mistakes which could have caused danger on the road.

Your examiner will help you by

- giving you a Driving Test Report form. This will show all the faults marked during the test and includes notes to explain the report
- explaining briefly why you haven't passed.

Listen to your examiner carefully. They will be able to help you by pointing out the aspects of your driving which you need to improve.

Study the Driving Test Report. It will include notes to help you understand how the examiner marks the form. You may then find it helpful to refer to the relevant sections in this book.

Show your copy of the report to your instructor, who will advise and help you to correct the faults. Listen to your instructor's advice carefully and get as much practice as you can. You can't take another test for at least 10 days.

Right of appeal – You'll obviously be disappointed if you don't pass your driving test. Although your examiner's decision can't be changed, if you think your test wasn't carried out according to the regulations, you have the right to appeal. If you live in England and Wales you have six months after the issue of the Statement of Failure in which to appeal (Magistrates' Courts Act 1952 Ch. 55 part VII, Sect. 104).

If you live in Scotland you have 21 days in which to appeal (Sheriff Court, Scotland Act of Sederunt (Statutory Appeals) 1981).

If you pass

Well done! You've shown that you can drive safely and confidently. Your examiner will give you a copy of the Driving Test Report which will show any driving faults which have been marked during the test and some notes to explain this report.

Your examiner will then ask for your provisional licence so that an upgraded licence can automatically be sent to you through the post.

Once the details have been taken, your examiner will keep your provisional licence and it will be securely destroyed. You will be given a pass certificate as proof of success until you receive your new licence.

If you don't want to surrender your licence you don't have to, and there will be certain circumstances when this isn't possible – for example, if you have changed your name.

In these cases you'll have to send your provisional licence, together with your pass certificate and the appropriate fee, to DVLA and it will send you your full licence. You have to do this within two years or you'll have to take your test again.

Look at the test report carefully and discuss it with your instructor. It includes notes to help you understand how the examiner marks the form.

You may then find it helpful to refer to the relevant sections in this book to help you overcome those weaknesses noted during your test.

Special rules under the New Drivers Act apply for the first two years after you have passed your test.

New Drivers Act

Your licence will be revoked if you receive six or more penalty points as a result of offences you commit within two years of passing your first practical test. This includes any offences you may have committed before passing your test.

> **Remember,** you will get a minimum of three penalty points for speeding – two speeding offences mean six points.

If you get six penalty points, you'll have your licence revoked and you must then reapply for a provisional licence. You'll then have to drive as a learner until you pass the theory and practical driving tests again. This applies even if you pay by fixed penalty.

For more information see **direct.gov.uk/newdriversact**

Pass Plus

Pass Plus is a training scheme for new drivers. Its aim is to improve your driving skills and make you a safer driver. It can also lead to insurance discounts.

The scheme has been designed by the Driving Standards Agency (DSA), with the help of the motor insurance and driving instruction industries, to develop your skills and knowledge in areas where you may have limited experience.

As an indicator of its effectiveness, a recent survey of practical test candidates (carried out by ORC International for DSA) showed that of those who had taken *Pass Plus*

- 93% felt more confident on the road
- 89% considered that their driving skills had improved.

This was as a result of taking the course.

> **Three ways to find out more**
>
> **1** Telephone **0115 936 6504**
>
> **2** Email **passplus@dsa.gsi.gov.uk**
>
> **3** Visit **direct.gov.uk/passplus**

* Subject to status. Candidates are advised to check available discounts with participating insurance companies – a full list can be found online at direct.gov.uk/passplus or by phoning 0115 936 6504.

What are the benefits?

Pass Plus will benefit you by

- enabling you to gain quality driving experience safely
- helping you to become a more skilful driver
- teaching you how to develop a positive driving style which is both enjoyable and safe
- reducing your risk of being involved in a road crash
- saving you money on your car insurance premiums.*

Pass Plus consists of a minimum of six hours' training and the emphasis is on developing your practical driving skills. There is no test at the end. Instead, you'll be assessed throughout: you must cover all the modules to complete the training.

Enjoy the course!

Saving money on your car insurance should bring a smile to your face.

Developing your driving skills

Motorway driving

It's important that you understand the rules and regulations of the motorway. However, as a learner you won't have been able to put the theory into practice – driving on the motorway for the first time can be a daunting experience.

If you take *Pass Plus*, one of the modules relates solely to motorway driving. Alternatively you can ask your instructor for motorway driving lessons where you will be able to gain valuable experience before you drive on your own on a motorway.

Further training

When you have successfully completed *Pass Plus* you will have demonstrated that you

- have developed your existing skills
- have acquired new skills and knowledge
- can drive safely in conditions not included in the driving test
- understand how you can reduce the risk of having a road traffic incident
- can maintain a courteous and considerate attitude to other road users.

Do you feel ready for the next level? If so, contact one of the organisations below.

DSA has approved and monitors advanced driving tests offered by

 The Institute of Advanced Motorists
Telephone 020 8996 9600
iam.org.uk

 DIAmond Advanced Motorists
Telephone 0845 345 5151
driving.org

 RoSPA Advanced Drivers' Association
Telephone 0121 248 2099
rospa.co.uk

 BSM Advanced Test
Telephone 01454 658 318
BSM.co.uk

section **five**
OTHER TESTS

This section covers
- Towing a trailer
- Retest for those who have lost their licence
- Assessment for taxi drivers

Towing a trailer

You must have a full car* driving licence before you can tow any trailer or caravan. The key factors that determine what licence you need are the maximum authorised mass (MAM)** of the car and trailer.

If you passed your test before 1 January 1997 you can drive a car towing a trailer or caravan.

If you passed your test after 1 January 1997

- you can tow a trailer less than 750 kg behind a car without taking a further test

- if you wish to tow a trailer larger than 750 kg you will normally have to take a further test (category B + E) – refer to DVLA factsheet 'Towing Trailers in Great Britain' which is available free of charge. Call **0300 790 6801** and quote INF30, or download direct from **direct.gov.uk/motoringleaflets.**

Further information

Detailed information and advice about towing trailers can be found in *The Official DSA Guide to Driving – the essential skills* which can be purchased from good bookshops or by calling **0870 241 4523.**

Useful information on towing can also be found on the following websites

- **ntta.co.uk** (The National Trailer and Towing Association Ltd)

- **caravanclub.co.uk**

- **campingandcaravanningclub.co.uk**

* A car includes any four-wheeled vehicle with a MAM of less than 3.5 tonnes which has no more than eight passenger seats.

** The MAM is the permissible maximum weight, also known as the gross vehicle weight.

If I don't fully load the trailer, can I tow a bigger one?

No, the size of trailer you can tow is dependent on the MAM, not the actual weight when loaded.

Do I have to take a theory test?

No, you have already passed a car theory test. There is no additional theory test for drivers towing trailers.

DVLA leaflet D100 contains comprehensive information about the licence you need to drive or tow any vehicle or trailer. D100 is available from **direct.gov.uk/motoringleaflets** as well as from Post Offices.

Key towing skills

You should consistently drive to the level detailed on pages 20-70; that is, to at least **Level 5** in the *Driver's Record*, the standard required to pass a car test. There are, however, some differences and these are explained here.

Safety checks (page 26)

You need to know how to carry out checks on the condition of the trailer body, check that any doors are secure and know how to load and secure a load to the trailer.
At the beginning of the test the examiner will ask you to explain or demonstrate five separate safety checks.

Mirrors (page 34)

You should know how to use additional mirrors and take relevant observation to compensate for the restricted view caused by large trailers and caravans.

Other traffic (page 42)

You should always show consideration for other road users by pulling up safely, when necessary, to allow others to pass and avoid the build up of queues of traffic behind you.

Turning the vehicle around (page 52)

The 'turn in the road' exercise isn't relevant to towing, but you need to know how to turn so you can travel in the opposite direction; for example, using a roundabout or side roads.

Reversing (page 54)

There will be a different exercise normally carried out at the beginning of the test. You will need to be able to reverse the car and trailer on a predetermined course to enter a restricted opening and then stop so that the extreme rear of the trailer is within a clearly defined area.

Parking (page 56)

During the test you won't be asked to carry out a reverse parking exercise while on the road.

Emergency stop (page 58)

There is no emergency stop for the B+E test, but you will have to carry out a braking exercise at the beginning of the test (see page 133).

Uncoupling and recoupling

You will also need to be able to uncouple and recouple your car and trailer. This is normally carried out at the end of the test (see page 136).

Practising

When you practise you must

- display L plates to the front of the car and the rear of the trailer. These must be clearly visible. You may use D plates in Wales if you wish
- be accompanied by a person who is at least 21 years old and holds a full EC/EEA driving licence for category B+E (they must have held this for the past three years).

You should also practise reversing and uncoupling/recoupling your car and trailer. You will be asked to do both these exercises as part of your test.

You should practise in all sorts of traffic conditions and on as many different roads as you can.

Practise turning left and right, taking into consideration the extra length of the unit. Be aware of your trailer, especially when taking sharp turns.

Booking and taking your test

Book your test as you would a car test (see page 115). However, be sure to make it clear that you want to take a B+E test.

The test can only take place at test centres for drivers of lorries and buses, where there is a manoeuvring area. To find out where these are, ask your trainer, call **0300 200 1122** or visit **direct.gov.uk/motoringnearest**

Also, as the test is longer there is a higher fee.

Documents

Make sure that you have your full licence with you and that it is signed. If your licence doesn't show your photograph you must have your passport with you (your passport doesn't have to be British).

Only licences issued in Great Britain or Northern Ireland are acceptable. Your examiner cannot conduct your test if you can't produce the correct documents.

Your test vehicle

The vehicle you intend to drive during your test should satisfy all the requirements given on pages 117-118 for those taking a car test. The L plates need to be displayed to the front of your car and the rear of your trailer. In addition, the vehicle should have an audible or visible warning device to confirm that the trailer indicator lights are operating.

Vehicle-trailer combinations should be fitted with nearside and offside externally mounted mirrors for use by the examiner.

Your test

Your test will include the following parts:

Eyesight check – Before you get into your car your examiner will point out a vehicle at a suitable distance and ask you to read its number plate. You must satisfy them that you can read the number plate as detailed on page 8. If you need glasses or contact lenses to read the number plate, that's fine, but you must wear them during the test and whenever you drive.

If you can't speak English or have difficulty reading, you may copy down what you see.

If your answer is incorrect, your examiner will measure the exact distance and repeat the test. If you fail the eyesight test, your test will go no further.

Safety check questions – The examiner will ask you to explain or demonstrate five separate safety checks.

Are there any minimum requirements for the trailer I'll be using during the test?

The unladen trailer must have a MAM of at least 1 tonne and the car and trailer together must be capable of 62.5 mph (100 km/h). If the car was registered after 1 October 2003, the trailer must have a closed box body.

What happens if I forget my documents?

If you don't have the correct documents or you forget to bring them with you, your test will be cancelled and you will lose your fee.

Extendable towing mirrors enable you to see what's behind you, rather than just seeing the side of the trailer or caravan.

Braking exercise – For safety reasons this will take place on a special manoeuvring area.

- Your examiner will point out two marker cones approximately 200 feet (61 metres) ahead
- You will be asked to build up speed so that you're travelling at about 20 mph as you reach the cones
- When the front of your car passes between the two markers, apply the brakes.

You should stop your car and trailer as quickly and as safely as possible, keeping full control and stopping in a straight line.

Don't drive too slowly or brake before you reach the marker points.

The drive – This will be approximately one hour long. It will include a wide variety of roads and traffic conditions including roads carrying two-way traffic, dual carriageways and, where possible, one-way systems and motorways.

Your examiner will expect you to drive at least to Level 5 standard and demonstrate all the key skills required in the car test. However, during the drive you won't be asked to

- do an emergency stop exercise on the road
- reverse around a corner
- reverse park
- turn in the road.

Make sure that you negotiate all hazards and junctions safely by using good, all-round observation.

All practical driving tests include approximately 10 minutes of independent driving during which you will be asked to drive either by following signs, a series of verbal directions or a combination of both.

Reversing exercise – This may take place at the beginning or end of the test. For full details of the reversing exercise see page 134.

Uncoupling and recoupling exercise – For full details of the uncoupling and recoupling exercise see page 136.

The reversing exercise

The reversing exercise for this test will usually take place before you leave the test centre and you will have to demonstrate that you can manoeuvre your car and trailer in a restricted space and stop at a specified point.

To carry out this part of the test you should be able to reverse your car and trailer in a restricted space.

Your examiner will ask you to drive forward before you begin to reverse.

You should be able to do this inside a clearly defined area

- under control and in reasonable time
- with good observation
- with reasonable accuracy.

Your examiner will show you a diagram of the manoeuvring area and explain what is required. The size of the reversing area will be set out according to the size of your car and trailer together as a unit

- cones A and A1 are positioned so they are 1 metre (just over 3 feet) into the area from the boundary line
- distance A to A1 is one-and-a-half times the width of the widest part of the unit
- A to B is twice the length of the car and trailer
- the overall length of the manoeuvring area will be five times the length of the car and trailer
- the width of the bay will be one-and-a-half times the widest part of the unit
- the length of the bay will be based on the overall length of the car and trailer as a unit but can be varied at the discretion of your examiner. This will be within the range of plus 1 metre or minus 2 metres but the precise length of the bay won't be disclosed before the start of the exercise.

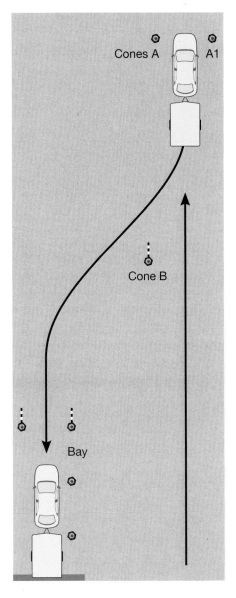

Tips from the experts

Approach cones A and A1 in a straight line and make sure that you stop at the cones; don't go too fast and go past them.

Turn the steering wheel the correct way as you start to reverse.

Keep in full control; don't let your wheel go over the yellow boundary or allow any part of your car to hit any of the cones or poles.

Use good all-round observation throughout the manoeuvre.

Make sure you stop so that the rear of your car and trailer is within the yellow box.

What to expect on test

You will be asked to

- drive forward and stop at a fixed point with the extreme front of your car level with, and in between, the cones A and A1

- reverse so that you pass cone B on the offside of your car

- stop so that the extreme rear of your trailer is within the painted yellow box area at the end of the bay

Uncoupling and recoupling

You will need to be able to uncouple the car and trailer, park the car and then recouple the two safely. You need to gain the skills to do this safely before you drive with a trailer on your own.

When uncoupling you first of all need to find a safe place with firm and level ground on which to carry out the procedure. Then you should

- ensure that the brakes are applied on both the car and the trailer (there are various parking mechanisms fitted to trailers; you should consult your manufacturer's handbook to ensure you operate these safely)
- ensure that the jockey wheel, legs or other device provided for supporting the trailer after uncoupling are lowered correctly. If there is any risk, strong planks or metal load spreaders should be used to distribute the weight
- disconnect the electric line(s) and stow away safely
- remove any fitted stabilising equipment
- remove any safety chain or coupling and move the trailer clear of the car.

When recoupling you should treat the trailer as a new trailer that you have not used before. You should

- ensure the brakes are correctly applied to the trailer
- move the car so that the trailer can be safely and easily coupled to it, and apply the parking brake
- attach the trailer to the car and check that the coupling is secure by using a method appropriate to the car and the trailer
- attach any safety chain or device
- fit any necessary stabilising equipment
- connect the electric line(s)
- ensure that the wheels, legs or other supporting devices are raised and secured safely
- check the operation of the lights and indicators and make sure the correct number plate is fitted
- release the trailer brake, ensuring that the car's parking brake is firmly applied.

What to expect on test

You will normally be asked to uncouple and recouple your car and trailer at the test centre at the end of the test.

Your examiner will ask you to stop where there is safe and level ground and then uncouple your car from the trailer. You will then be asked to park the car alongside the trailer before realigning the car with the trailer and recoupling the two. Your examiner will expect you to make sure that the

- coupling is secure
- lights and indicators are operating
- trailer brake is released.

When uncoupling or recoupling make sure the brake is correctly applied before you start.

Tips from the experts

Make sure that you carry out the procedure in the correct sequence, and that you can do it confidently and without hesitating.

When uncoupling, make sure you have applied the brakes to both the car and trailer before you start and don't release the trailer coupling without the wheels or legs being lowered.

Don't try to move forward until the whole uncoupling procedure has been completed.

When recoupling, make sure that the brakes are applied on the trailer and that you use good, effective all round observation as you reverse.

Don't try to move away without raising the wheels or legs and checking the lights, indicators, safety chain and trailer brake release.

Make sure that the jockey wheel is lowered after uncoupling and then raised and secured safely when recoupling.

Retest for those who have lost their licence

Losing your licence

If you lose your licence after being convicted of a driving offence, you may have to take a normal-length or extended driving test before you can recover your full licence.

The court can impose the following penalties

- an extended driving test on anyone convicted of dangerous driving offences (this is an obligatory penalty)
- an extended driving test on anyone convicted of other offences involving obligatory disqualification
- a normal-length driving test for other endorsable offences.

If you've been given one of these penalties, you can apply for a provisional licence at the end of the disqualification period.

If your licence has been revoked under the New Drivers Act (see page 125) you will also have to apply for a new provisional licence.

Provisional licence

The normal rules for provisional licence holders apply:

- you must be supervised by a person who is at least 21 years old and has held a full driving licence for the category of vehicle being driven for the past three years
- the car must display L plates (or D plates in Wales) to the front and rear
- you're not allowed to drive on motorways.

You will have to pass the theory test before you can apply to take your practical driving test again. You should study the training materials before you take the test (see page 16).

Once you have passed the theory test, you can then apply to take your practical test.

Extended test

An extended test covers a wide variety of roads, usually including dual carriageways. This test is marked and assessed at the same level as a normal practical test, but is more demanding due to the longer time devoted to normal driving. Make sure that you're ready.

> **Remember,** the extended test lasts about 70 minutes. This is half an hour longer than the standard practical car test.

You're advised to take suitable instruction from an instructor.

You have to pay a higher fee for this test because of the longer duration.

What to expect on test – In addition to the longer drive detailed above, your test will include all the exercises included in the normal test.

You will be asked to carry out one exercise using your car's reverse gear. That may be

- reversing round a corner
- turning in the road
- reverse parking (either in a bay at the test centre or on the side of the road).

Your examiner will ask you to pull up, and will then explain the exercise and ask you to carry it out. The examiner will select which one at random, so you should be prepared to demonstrate any one of them.

You will also be asked to carry out an emergency stop during the test.

There will be approximately 10 minutes of independent driving during which you will be asked to drive by following signs, following a series of verbal directions or a combination of both.

Your examiner will watch you and, in addition to the normal observations detailed throughout the key skills, will also take account of your ability to concentrate for the duration of the test and your attitude to other road users.

Assessment for taxi drivers

Throughout this section 'hackney carriages' and 'private hire vehicles' will be referred to as 'taxis' and their drivers as 'taxi drivers'.

Licensing requirements

You must have a full car licence. Check with your local authority to find out if they require a DSA taxi assessment. If they do, you should be given an information pack by the licensing authority and you will have to apply to DSA to get an appointment for your assessment.

Further information

Detailed information and advice about taxi driving can be found in *The Official DSA Guide to Driving – the essential skills* which can be purchased from bookshops, online at **tsoshop.co.uk/dsa** or by mail order by calling **0870 241 4523**.

Key skills

The basic skills you will be expected to show are detailed in the main part of this book, on pages 21-70.

However, the examiner will also take into account that you are an experienced driver and therefore will expect you to demonstrate a greater degree of skill and road sense associated with that

You'll have to demonstrate that you're a competent and considerate driver and not a danger to yourself or to any other road user.

of an experienced driver. For example, because of your experience you should be able to take advantage of gaps in the traffic to emerge safely at road junctions where a learner driver may hesitate.

The level of ability required will be higher than that of a learner driving test and will take into account issues specifically related to taxi driving. The emphasis will be on road safety and the safe conveyance of passengers.

You must ensure at all times that your passenger feels safe and comfortable during their journey. This includes the care of your passengers as you pick them up and drop them off at their destination in a safe and convenient place.

Taxi manoeuvring exercise – For this you have to turn your vehicle around in the road in the most appropriate manner. This is because, as a taxi driver, you may often have to carry out a manoeuvre such as this.

You will be asked to carry out this exercise on a section of road where there are various options open to you. It is up to you to choose the safest and most appropriate method for the road and traffic conditions.

You may be able to consider and choose from

- a turn in the road
- a left or right reverse
- a 'U' turn.

When doing this

- you may be able to use the larger area available at the mouth of a junction in which to swing round
- never reverse from a side road into a main road – it is very dangerous
- make sure you don't hit the kerb and don't use private driveways.

Stopping at the side of the road – You are likely to have to do this more often than most drivers, so you will be asked to carry out two or three stops as if dropping off or picking up a passenger.

When doing this

- pull up at a reasonable distance from the kerb where it is safe, legal and convenient to do so

On your assessment, choose a place to stop where a passenger – if you had one – could open the door fully and easily leave the taxi.

- apply the handbrake and put the gear into neutral
- make sure that if you had passengers there is nothing to stop them opening the door easily, such as trees or street furniture.

All practical driving tests include approximately 10 minutes of independent driving during which you will be asked to drive by following signs, following a series of verbal directions or a combination of both.

If you are planning to take the additional part of the assessment which enables you to carry wheelchairs, there will be an exercise at the end of the assessment to check that you can safely load and unload a wheelchair.

Booking and taking your assessment

Book your assessment as you would a car test (see page 115). However, be sure to let them know that you need a taxi assessment and the type of assessment you want to take. The types of taxi assessment available are as follows

- all saloon vehicles/Hackney carriage saloon (this is known as a 'Z' assessment)
- Hackney carriage (drive and wheelchair) – black cab or MPV with wheelchair facilities (this is known as a 'Z1' assessment)
- Hackney carriage wheelchair assessment only (this is known as a 'Z2' assessment).

Documents – Make sure that you have your full licence with you and that it is signed. If your licence doesn't show your photograph you must have your passport with you (your passport doesn't have to be British).

Only licences issued in Great Britain or Northern Ireland are acceptable. Your examiner cannot conduct your assessment if you can't produce the correct documents.

Your assessment vehicle – Your vehicle needs to comply with all the regulations for a learner test (see pages 117-118), except that it shouldn't display L plates.

Your assessment

Your assessment will include the following parts.

Eyesight test – At the start of your assessment your examiner will test your eyesight by asking you to read a vehicle number plate (see pages 10 and 120). If you are only taking the wheelchair assessment you will not have to do the eyesight test.

Can I take my assessment at any test centre?

The taxi assessment can only take place at certain centres. The wheelchair assessment can only take place at some of these centres. Appropriate centres are shown on the application form, but there should always be a centre within easy reach of your licensing authority home town.

Will I be asked any safety check questions?

There will be no safety check questions at the beginning of the assessment. However, at the end of the assessment you will have to answer some Highway Code/Cabology questions (see the opposite page for further information).

The drive – This will be approximately 40 minutes. It will include a wide variety of roads and traffic conditions including roads carrying two-way traffic, dual carriageways and, where possible, one-way systems and motorways.

It is important that you drive as naturally as possible. Don't try to adjust your driving to what you may feel an examiner would expect to see – drive as you would normally.

The examiner will sit in the front passenger seat of a saloon car, but in a black cab style hackney carriage they will sit in the back and ask you to either open the sliding glass screen or turn on the intercom system.

You will be asked five questions about traffic signs at the end of your assessment.

The major part of the assessment will be carried out in a similar way to that of the learner driver test (pages 117-118). However, one of the special exercises will be the special taxi manoeuvring exercise.

Highway Code and Cabology – At the end of the assessment you will be asked a number of questions

- three questions on *The Official Highway Code*
- two cabology questions – these are questions about the safety of the vehicle (tyres and safety features), and your responsibilities as a taxi driver for the safety of your passengers. In addition, black cab drivers may also be asked about the dimensions of their vehicle
- five traffic sign questions.

Wheelchair exercise
See page 145.

143

Tips from the experts

You must drive to at least the standard set out on pages 20-67. Because you are an experienced driver, many of the skills you need to show will be second nature. Also, because you are an experienced driver, make sure that you are aware of the following points

- When you manoeuvre, make sure that your vehicle is under control at all times and that you take good all round observation throughout the manoeuvre. Always consider other road users and pedestrians.

- When pulling away from a stationary position at the side of the road, remember to look over your shoulder to check your blind spot before pulling away.

- Use all your mirrors (interior and exterior) effectively and at the appropriate times so you can demonstrate that you are aware of what is happening around your vehicle at all times.

- Signal correctly and in good time to let other road users see and understand what you plan to do.

- You understand and comply with all traffic signs and road markings and that you see and react to signals given by the police, traffic wardens and other road users.

- You make good progress, within the speed limit, when the road and traffic conditions enable you to do so.

- Watch your separation distance from the vehicle in front and also from parked cars.

- Use sound judgement and planning when you overtake, meet oncoming vehicles and turn right in front of oncoming traffic. Never cause another vehicle to brake or swerve to avoid you.

Plan ahead; try to predict how the actions of other road users and pedestrians will affect your driving and react in good time.

How your assessment is marked

Your assessment is marked by the examiner in a similar way to that described on page 122 and the examiner will use similar criteria to those explained on that page. However, if you commit 10 or more driving faults you will fail the assessment.

The wheelchair exercise

You need to be able to load a wheelchair safely, make sure that it is secured as if for a journey, and then unload it safely.

The wheelchair will be provided by DSA. This will be an empty wheelchair; remember that it will handle differently from one in which a person is seated.

What the assessment requires – You will be asked to

- securely erect the wheelchair ramps
- safely install the wheelchair in your vehicle, backing the chair to the fold-down seats. Secure both wheelchair brakes
- secure seat belt/safety harness and also secure wheel belts/clamps if they are fitted to your vehicle
- satisfy yourself that the wheelchair is secure, as you would before starting a journey, then reverse the whole procedure.

Tips from the experts

Make sure the ramp is locked securely in place before attempting to wheel the chair inside. If the ramp is in more than one section, make sure that the sections are locked together correctly and do not spring apart once pressure is released.

Both brakes need to be fully applied in the locked position. This requires a certain amount of pressure and the brake pad should be fully depressed into the tyre.

Ensure that the harness is fixed to the main tubular frame of the wheelchair.

Check all the brakes, harness and seatbelts are secure before advising the examiner that you've finished.

Always walk out backwards when you're wheeling the chair out of the vehicle, it's dangerous to push the chair in front of you.

annex one
Service standards

We judge our performance against the following standards (printed in our Business Plan) which we review each year

- We will provide a full response to enquiries quickly - we will respond to 90% of general enquiries within 10 working days.

- We will provide a full response to complaints quickly - we will respond to 90% of complaints within 10 working days.

- We will respond to telephone calls promptly and endeavour to resolve all enquiries at the first call - we will answer 70% of telephone calls within 30 seconds.

- We will give 95% of candidates an appointment at their preferred theory test centre within two weeks of their preferred date.

- We will keep 99.5% of all theory test appointments.

- We will keep 98% of practical test appointments that are in place three days prior to the test.

- National average waiting time for practical car tests will be no longer than six weeks.

Complaints guide

DSA aims to give its customers the best possible service. Please tell us when we have done well or if you're not satisfied.

Your comments can help us to improve the service we offer.

If you have any questions about how your test was conducted, please contact the local supervising examiner, whose address is displayed at your local driving test centre.

If you are dissatisfied with the reply or you wish to comment on other matters, you can write to DSA.

If your concern relates to an ADI you should write to

The Registrar of Approved Driving Instructors
Driving Standards Agency
The Axis Building
112 Upper Parliament Street
Nottingham NG1 6LP

Finally, you can write to

The Chief Executive
Driving Standards Agency
The Axis Building
112 Upper Parliament Street
Nottingham NG1 6LP

None of this removes your right to take your complaint to

- your Member of Parliament, who may decide to raise your case personally with the DSA Chief Executive, the Minister, or the Parliamentary Commissioner for Administration (the Ombudsman) (see page 3)
- a magistrates' court (in Scotland, to the Sheriff of your area) if you believe that your test wasn't carried out according to the regulations.

Before doing this, you should seek legal advice.

Refunding fees and expenses

DSA always aims to keep test appointments, but occasionally it has to cancel a test at short notice. DSA will refund the test fee, or give you your next test free, in the following circumstances

- if DSA cancels a test
- if you cancel a test and give DSA at least three working days' notice (Saturday is counted as a working day)
- if you keep the test appointment but the test doesn't take place or isn't finished, for a reason that isn't your fault or the fault of the vehicle you are using.

DSA will also compensate you for the money you lost if it cancelled your test at short notice (unless it was for bad weather).

For example, DSA will pay

- the cost of hiring a vehicle for the test, including reasonable travelling time to and from the test centre
- any pay or earnings you lost, after tax and so on (usually for half a day).

DSA *won't* pay the cost of driving lessons which you arrange linked to a particular test appointment, or extra lessons you decide to take while waiting for a rescheduled test.

How to apply – Please write to the DSA Enquiries and Booking Centre and send a receipt showing hire car charges, or an employer's letter which shows what earnings you lost. If possible, please use the standard form (available from every driving test centre or booking office) to make your claim.

These arrangements don't affect your legal rights.

annex two
Private practice record

When you go out driving with a friend or relative, DSA would encourage you to record the type of driving experience that you have gained.

You can use these forms to record what you did by ticking the appropriate boxes. You'll probably tick several for each drive; for example, it may have been light when you started to drive but dark by the time you finished. Take note of the time and mileage when you start so that you can fill in how much time you spent on the road and how many miles you covered.

Fill in the time in hours (0.5 hours) and the distance in miles (20 miles). Visit **direct.gov.uk/driversrecord** for further information and to download copies of these forms.

Date	Wet roads	Dry roads	Darkness	Daylight	Dual carriageway	Country	Town and city	Overall time	Distance travelled	Comments
	◯	◯	◯	◯	◯	◯	◯	◯	◯	
	◯	◯	◯	◯	◯	◯	◯	◯	◯	
	◯	◯	◯	◯	◯	◯	◯	◯	◯	
	◯	◯	◯	◯	◯	◯	◯	◯	◯	
	◯	◯	◯	◯	◯	◯	◯	◯	◯	
	◯	◯	◯	◯	◯	◯	◯	◯	◯	
	◯	◯	◯	◯	◯	◯	◯	◯	◯	

Date	Wet roads	Dry roads	Darkness	Daylight	Dual carriageway	Country	Town and city	**Overall time**	**Distance travelled**	Comments

Date	Wet roads	Dry roads	Darkness	Daylight	Dual carriageway	Country	Town and city	**Overall time**	**Distance travelled**	Comments
	☐	☐	☐	☐	☐	☐	☐	☐	☐	
	☐	☐	☐	☐	☐	☐	☐	☐	☐	
	☐	☐	☐	☐	☐	☐	☐	☐	☐	
	☐	☐	☐	☐	☐	☐	☐	☐	☐	
	☐	☐	☐	☐	☐	☐	☐	☐	☐	
	☐	☐	☐	☐	☐	☐	☐	☐	☐	
	☐	☐	☐	☐	☐	☐	☐	☐	☐	
	☐	☐	☐	☐	☐	☐	☐	☐	☐	
	☐	☐	☐	☐	☐	☐	☐	☐	☐	
	☐	☐	☐	☐	☐	☐	☐	☐	☐	
	☐	☐	☐	☐	☐	☐	☐	☐	☐	
	☐	☐	☐	☐	☐	☐	☐	☐	☐	
	☐	☐	☐	☐	☐	☐	☐	☐	☐	
	☐	☐	☐	☐	☐	☐	☐	☐	☐	
	☐	☐	☐	☐	☐	☐	☐	☐	☐	
	☐	☐	☐	☐	☐	☐	☐	☐	☐	
	☐	☐	☐	☐	☐	☐	☐	☐	☐	
	☐	☐	☐	☐	☐	☐	☐	☐	☐	
	☐	☐	☐	☐	☐	☐	☐	☐	☐	
	☐	☐	☐	☐	☐	☐	☐	☐	☐	
	☐	☐	☐	☐	☐	☐	☐	☐	☐	

Date	Wet roads	Dry roads	Darkness	Daylight	Dual carriageway	Country	Town and city	**Overall time**	**Distance travelled**	Comments

Other Official DSA Publications

The Official DSA Guide to Hazard Perception DVD

Hazard perception is a vital skill and a key part of today's driving tests. This interactive DVD from the Driving Standards Agency will help you stay safe on the roads.

Includes official DSA video clips to develop and test your responses to hazards.

ISBN 9780115528651   **£15.99**

Prepare for your Practical Driving Test – the official DSA guide DVD

Taking away the mystery of what actually happens during your practical driving test, this is the only official interactive DVD which clearly shows you how to reach Level 5 – the practical test pass standard – for each of the 24 key driving skills examined in the test. Includes new information on independent driving.

ISBN 9780115531446   **£15.99**

facebook
Visit our Facebook page at **facebook.com/learningtodrive**

twitter
Follow us on Twitter **twitter.com/DSA_Publishers**

information & publishing solutions

The **OFFICIAL DSA GUIDE** to
LEARNING
TO DRIVE

2011 WIN A CAR COMPETITION*

TSO, DSA's official publishing partner, is offering you the chance to win a new car.

To enter, simply answer the questions and tell us in 25 words or less how learning to drive will make a difference to your life. The winner will be the entrant who answers the first 3 questions correctly and writes the most apt and original 25 word essay, as decided by the judges.

Please send the entry form to: Win a Car Competition 2011, TSO, Freepost, ANG 4748, Norwich, NR3 1YX (No stamp required). Closing date: 5 September 2011.

1. **You may only use front fog lights when visibility is reduced to less than what distance?**

....

2. **What is the legal minimum insurance cover you must have to drive on public roads?**

....

3. **When may you drive over a footpath?**

....

Tie Breaker: Learning to drive will change my life... (complete in 25 words or less)

....

....

....

....

* Terms and conditions apply

When are you planning/hoping to take your theory test?

Within a fortnight ☐ Within a month ☐ In 1-3 months ☐ In 3-6 months ☐
In 6-12 months ☐ In 12+ months ☐

When are you planning/hoping to take your practical test?

Within a fortnight ☐ Within a month ☐ In 1-3 months ☐ In 3-6 months ☐
In 6-12 months ☐ in 12+ months ☐

Do you already own a car?

Yes ☐ No ☐

If Yes, is the car...

New ☐ Second-hand ☐

Do you plan to buy a car when you pass?

Yes ☐ No ☐

If Yes, will the car be...

New ☐ Second-hand ☐

Name of shop or website that you bought this product from?

....

How would you improve this, or any other DSA product?

....

....

Name ....

Address ....

.... Date of birth ....

Daytime tel. .... Email ....

Mobile tel. ....

TSO (The Stationery Office) Ltd is proud to be DSA's official publishing partner

Prices, images and publication dates are correct at time of going to press but may be subject to change without notice.

Account holders should note that all credit card transactions will not be shown on their statements. The personal information provided here will only be used to process your order and keep you informed of related products or services. We will not pass your data on to any third parties.

TSO would like to continue to keep you informed of products and services that may be of interest to you. If you do not wish to receive these updates in future please let us know.

I do not want to receive these updates from TSO in the future ☐

I have read, accept and agree to be bound by the Competition Rules

Signature .... Date ....

If you would like us to send you email updates on your specific area(s) of interest register at tsoshop.co.uk/signup

Competition Rules

The following rules apply to this competition. By entering this competition, entrants will be deemed to have accepted these rules and to agree to be bound by them.

1. Only one entry will be accepted per purchase of The Official DSA Guide to Learning to Drive.

2. All entries must be on original official entry forms. No photocopies will be accepted.

3. Entries must be received by the Promoter by no later than 5.00pm on Monday, 5 September 2011 (**Closing Date**). Entries must be submitted by ordinary post to the Promoter's free mailing address at: TSO, Freepost, ANG 4748, Norwich, NR3 1YX.

4. The competition will run from 12 July 2010 to 5 September 2011 and one prize shall be awarded to a winner chosen from valid entries received by the Promoter by the Closing Date. No responsibility can be taken by the Promoter for lost, late, misdirected or stolen entries.

5. The prize awarded to the winner will be one car (not necessarily the car pictured), being either a Peugeot 107 Urban Lite 1.0 three door Petrol model or another make and model of approximate equivalent value (manufacturer's RRP of £7,793 at the time of these rules going to press) to be selected by the Promoter in its absolute discretion. Colour is subject to availability. Insurance and all on the road charges are not included and will be the winner's responsibility. There will be one prize only and accordingly only one winner. The prize cannot be transferred or exchanged and there is no cash alternative.

6. Only entrants over the age of 17 and resident in the United Kingdom are eligible to enter the competition. The Promoter reserves the right to request evidence of proof of age and residence from the winner before any prize will be awarded.

7. The winning entry will be decided by the judges in their absolute discretion from correct entries submitted by eligible entrants received by the Closing Date. A "correct" entry means a fully completed entry, with the first three questions answered correctly, the most apt and original essay and otherwise in compliance with these rules.

8. The winner will be notified by 23 September 2011. Only the winner will be contacted personally via the email address or telephone number they provide.

9. If the winner cannot be contacted by the means provided, the Promoter reserves the right to have the judges decide on an alternative winner from other correct entries received by the Closing Date, using the same criteria as for the original "winner" and subject to these rules.

10. The winner's name will be published on the Promoter's website at www.tso.co.uk on or about 23 September 2011 for a period of approximately 60 days.

11. The prize will be made available within six weeks of the Closing Date by arrangement between the Promoter and the winner, provided that the Promoter shall not be responsible for any delivery costs.

12. By entering this competition, an entrant agrees that if they accept any Prize, they will be deemed to consent to:

    (a) the use for promotional and other purposes (without further payment and except as prohibited by law) of their name, city/town/county of residence, likeness and Prize information; and

    (b) participate in the Promoter's reasonable marketing and promotional activities.

    The entrant agrees that all rights including copyright in all works created by the entrant as part of the competition entry shall be owned by the Promoter absolutely without the need for any payment to the entrant. They further agree to waive unconditionally and irrevocably all moral rights pursuant to the Copyright, Designs and Patents Act of 1988 and under any similar law in force from time to time anywhere in the world in respect of all such works.

13. No entries will be returned to entrants by the Promoter. Therefore, entrants may wish to retain a copy.

14. The Promoter reserves the right to cancel this competition or amend these rules at any stage without prior notice, if deemed necessary in its opinion, especially if circumstances arise outside of its control. Any such cancellation or changes to the rules will be notified on the Promoter's website.

15. This competition is not open to employees or contractors of the Promoter or the Driving Standards Agency or any person directly involved in the organisation or running of the competition, or their direct family members. Any such entries will be invalid.

16. By entering this competition, entrants warrant that all information submitted by them is true and correct and that they are eligible and have legal capacity to enter this competition. The Promoter reserves the right to disqualify any entrant if it has reasonable grounds to believe that the entrant has breached these rules.

17. Any personal data provided in any entry will be dealt with by the Promoter in accordance with the requirements of the Data Protection Act 1998, provided that the winner expressly consents to the information set out in rule 12(a) being used in the manner specified therein.

18. The judges' and the Promoter's decisions in relation to any aspect of this competition are final and no correspondence will be entered into. Neither the judges nor the Promoter will have any liability to any person in relation to their decisions or any damage, loss, injury or disappointment suffered arising from the competition (except to the extent that such liability cannot be limited or excluded by law).

19. The competition and these rules shall be governed by English law.

20. The "Promoter" means The Stationery Office Limited, St Crispins, Duke Street, Norwich, NR3 1PD (the publishers of The Official DSA Learner Range). The competition judging panel will be made up of a combination of the Promoter's employees and independent judge(s).

Other Official DSA Publications

The Official DSA Guide to Driving – the essential skills
Book   ISBN 9780115531347   £12.99
Downloadable PDF   ISBN 9780115531385   £12.99*

The industry standard driving manual packed with advice for learners, professional drivers and instructors. Includes guidance on essential driving techniques, manoeuvring and defensive driving.

The Official DSA Theory Test for Car Drivers and The Official Highway Code
Book   ISBN 9780115531262   £12.99
CD-ROM   ISBN 9780115531286   £12.99
Downloadable PDF   ISBN 9780115531361   £12.99*

Includes every theory test question you could be asked until January 2012, together with the full DSA explanation of the answers and The Official Highway Code. Includes practice for case studies and references from every question to the official source material. The CD-ROM provides the closest experience to the multiple choice part of the theory test and includes a useful voice-over option.

The Official DSA Complete Theory Test Kit – CD-ROM and DVD
ISBN 9780115531309   £19.99

Prepare for both parts of the theory test. Includes Theory Test for Car Drivers CD-ROM and Hazard Perception DVD. This Theory Test CD-ROM contains all the theory test questions you could be asked until January 2012. Save £8.99 on individual prices.

The Official DSA Complete Learner Driver Pack – electronic version
ISBN 9780115531323   £29.99

Provides complete preparation for your theory and practical tests. Includes Theory Test for Car Drivers CD-ROM, Hazard Perception DVD and Prepare for your Practical Driving Test DVD. This Theory Test CD-ROM contains all the theory test questions you could be asked until January 2012. Save £14.98 on individual prices.

TSO (The Stationery Office) is proud to be DSA's official publishing partner.

6 Easy Ways To Order:

Online: Visit tsoshop.co.uk/dsa
Email: Email your order to dsa.merchandising@tso.co.uk
Telephone: Please call 0870 850 6553 and quote reference CQD
Fax: Fax your order to 0870 243 0129
Post: Marketing, TSO, Freepost, ANG 4748, Norwich NR3 1YX (No stamp required)
Shops: Available from all good High Street book stores (including the TSO shop) or online book stores. For interactive products please also visit selected computer software retailers.

Prices, covers and publication dates are correct at time of going to press but may be subject to change without notice.

*PDF downloads provide immediate access at the press of a button. Available direct from TSO – visit tsoshop.co.uk/PDF